Dedicated to my family. My parents who have inspired me with their unwavering love and support. My wife Kate, and kids Kayla and Nate, who teach me the joys of being a family and also keep me grounded.

Finally, I am grateful to my awesome colleagues and friends that I have worked with over the years. You are an extraordinary group who helped collaborate and reinforce materials in this book. When you read the pages, you will know your part.

Contents

Forward by Jason Latonio

Enterprise Architecture is often looked at as an ivory tower: an unobtainable, expensive, and bureaucratic practice whose value is not well understood. Riddled with complex frameworks and methodologies, an Enterprise Architecture practice can be difficult to get off the ground or learn if you are just getting started.

Enterprise Architecture does not need to be complicated, in fact, Russ Gibfried has developed a practical and pragmatic approach to delivering Enterprise Architecture to any size organization. I know. I worked with Russ for two years and he has tuned EA methods into a playbook that you can follow either as an EA Leader, or as a technical contributor. In this book, Russ steps you through how to communicate and deliver the value of EA in easy to understand terms and language. With this you can unlock new efficiencies within Information Technology by lowering ongoing costs, improving speed to market, knowledge sharing, project execution, and helping establish a common vision for IT.

If you are an IT Leader that is looking to or have started an EA practice, this book can help you put together a plan for communicating the service offerings for EA, as well as a phased approach for introducing them into your organization. If you are an aspiring Enterprise Architect, this book will help you understand what skills, experience, and character traits are necessary to become a successful and effective. Russ has a knack for making things simple, practical, and easy to understand. He has taken his many years of experience as an Enterprise Architecture leader, extracted the most useful and practical nuggets from that experience, and created an EA playbook to implement Enterprise Architecture in any organization.

Preface | Is this book for me?

Confucius, the well-known Chinese philosopher once said, "I hear and I forget. I see and I remember. I do and I understand." Making a strong point about learning, Confucius expresses that true learning happens by doing and taking action, rather than just listening and watching. Although Confucius lived between 551-479 BC, Confucian values influence business practices today by extolling hard work, thrift and resource efficiency to attain results in productivity and profitability. One of the areas we see Confucian values in Western capitalism is Information Technology (IT) and Enterprise Architecture (EA).

EA initially began in the 1960s as Business System Planning, but evolved and took hold in the 1990s when companies started using EA as a framework to model business technology. They were successful and the modern Enterprise Architecture (EA) discipline was set in motion[1]. As Gartner® defines EA, it is "a discipline for proactively and holistically leading enterprise responses to disruptive forces by identifying and analyzing the execution of change toward desired business vision and outcomes." With all due respect to Gartner, Confucius would say, "I hear and I forget".

In more understandable terms, EA is about developing an Information Technology (IT) blueprint which not only effectively meets your organization's current business needs but also proactively anticipates and prepares for its future ones. For the EA practitioner, it requires technical knowledge, data analytic skills, and business acumen to chart an IT strategic vision aligned with business objectives. With the goal to reduce costs and increase organizational productivity, EA navigates a path through necessary levels of business process integration, standardization and security.

Gartner is a registered trademark and service mark of Gartner, Inc.

However, the need for a traditional EA practice can swing like a pendulum. Traditional EA programs can often seem static, based on Visio® and PowerPoints® that are time stamped. Without perceived immediate value, interest in EA wanes and the practice can dissolve like a melting iceberg. While the business moves and transforms daily to support customer needs, EA materials are dated and fixed. But what if EA could tap into wells of IT information and visibly link the company's capabilities, business processes, data objects and applications; creating a real-time picture of the enterprise? What if EA (and IT) could flex and scale at the rate to meet business demand? This would be dynamic and would allow business leaders to demand action based on real-time data that EA cultivates and transforms directly into actionable insights. This book is your guide for <u>doing and taking action in creating a dynamic living Enterprise Architecture</u> based on reference frameworks, impactful deliverables and tuned data-driven models; allowing IT and the business to deliver consistent positive results. This book, and its three parts: **Strategic Frameworks**, **Tactical Deliverables** and **The Living Architecture** will enhance your Enterprise Architecture career and your company's prospects. As Confucius would, "I do and I understand."

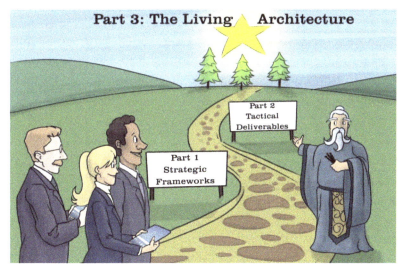

CONFUCIUS, "I HEAR AND I FORGET. I SEE AND I REMEMBER. I DO AND I UNDERSTAND."

Microsoft®, Microsoft Visio® and Microsoft Powerpoint® are trademarks of the Microsoft group of companies.

Is this book for me?

Before my introduction to EA, my career started as a software developer doing low-level development and data integration. At various times, I was an employee, consultant and business owner responsible for projects in a broad-spectrum of industries (finance, defense, consumer goods, entertainment, energy, bio med, etc.). Everything was a stream of ones and zeros; I was at the top of my programming game. With my introduction to EA, I standardized my design approach and embraced the big picture from both an end-to-end business perspective and IT design. It enabled me to design better solutions, and more importantly, build consensus for designs that could be leveraged by larger teams. By utilizing a standard EA methodology, and techniques like Solution Designs and Whiteboarding Sessions, I was able to arrive at the best end-to-end solutions quicker with support from all stakeholders. If you are a technical contributor and want to get to the next level, this book is for you!

During my thirty years in technology, I have had the good fortune to work with some fantastic organizations and leaders; but not all organizations are right for an EA practice since EA takes a certain level of commitment and dedication. A good parallel is the concept of Pioneers, Settlers and Town Planners[2] introduced by researcher Simon Wardley. In this analogy, Pioneers venture into new territory while Settlers piggy-back on the work of Pioneers to standardize discoveries into a better functioning and more efficient products and/or services. Town Planners solidify and strengthen the work of both by streamlining and commoditizing the product or service to enable efficient mass consumption.

Pioneers (think of Lewis and Clark who charted the Oregon Trail from St. Louis to Oregon between 1803-1806) are companies that venture into new business territories and come up with exciting new ideas that can create or change a market. In a start-up company, an entrepreneurial spirit is needed because speed, flexibility and/or failure are a priority in order to discover the next best thing.

Settlers follow the pioneer's trail. These companies have found a product or service in a promising market. Settlers focus their energy on improving the product or service in order to meet the users' need – and earn profits.

Town Planners enter the cycle by specializing on increasing the product or service efficiency so it can be standardized, offered and consumed at scale. Just like the infrastructure and logistics to support a modern-day city, Town Planners standardize the entire product or service so it can be adopted and supported on a global scale.

If your business is in the Pioneer phases, then the hands-on materials in Part 2 will provide valuable help in getting ahead. Part 2 cuts through the theory in favor of tuned and actionable templatized deliverables. These templates help document and capture architecture decision points and technical designs to support a directional heading.

If you or your business is in the Settler or Town Planner phase, then this book is definitely for you! It is a hands-on, practical guide for applying Enterprise Architecture techniques – to create an Enterprise Architecture practice that enables business competitive advantage. EA is a broad and dense subject, typically consisting of current and future state architectures, gap analysis and knowledge of four key Architecture domains (Business, Information, Applications and Technology). Additionally, the Enterprise Architect must manage these by implementing policies and standards in order to achieve business goals and strategic direction. Without a proven Enterprise Architecture guidebook to draw from, most EA practices become overwhelmed and eventually labeled as "ivory towers" that pontificate standards and high-level strategy with little practical use. To deliver value, this book will show you how to operate Enterprise Architecture in two modes:

- **Strategic:** Providing actionable transformational (multi-year) guidance and planning that aligns IT and business capabilities to the overall company strategic vision.
- **Tactical:** Providing day-to-day hands-on IT execution and project support through EA artifacts like Solution Design Documents (SDDs),

Reference Patterns and Assessments. These provide the foundation and guardrails for project delivery and team execution.

How do I get the most from this book?

At the end of each chapter I have summarized the key points and real-life experiences as take-aways. These are the salient points and actual observations that you should remember. Take notes in the book and time to reflect. Although I have found the methods outlined essential, every company is slightly different and methods can be tuned for your specific scenario.

Implementing an EA program is a journey that takes time; approximately 1 -2 years for mid-sized companies and 2+ years for a large company. Read this book every six months to check your progress and note your shortcomings and successes. The web site **www.successful-ea.com** that accompanies this book, provides access to content and allows you to ask questions and contribute findings.

****

Take-Away

- ➤ If you are a Settler or Town Planner, implementing an Enterprise Architecture practice is an exciting journey. The techniques outlined in this book are industry proven, data driven and will help solidify the architecture practice to provide lasting organizational value. Proceed to Part 1.
- ➤ If you are a Pioneer or technical contributor, the hands-on Enterprise Architecture methods and materials will help you get ahead. Proceed to Part 2

****

****

PART ONE - Strategic Frameworks for a Successful EA Practice

Welcome to Part 1. This section will step through standard industry frameworks and methodologies which will be helpful in shaping and tuning the EA practice in further chapters. These frameworks are:

- o TOGAF® - Your Architecture Methodology (important in Part 2)
- o APQC® - For documenting business processes (important in Part 3)
- o CMMI® Maturity Model – To measure performance and value (important for your job)
- o EVM – Using data to predict project health (important in Part 2)

Chapter 1 - TOGAF: Your Architecture Methodology

A successful Enterprise Architecture practice enables business execution by creating a clear picture of the organization's IT Landscape (mapping technologies to business processes and capabilities). These mappings help downstream delivery teams execute the strategy necessary to transform from point A to point B. The architecture process involves considering the needs and requirements of the participating departments so that key drivers and issues can be detected in advance, synthesized and prioritized into appropriate workstreams. The Enterprise Architecture process provides the body of repeatable methods, processes and policies employed by the EA team to govern and guide the organization to be highly functional and adaptable in supporting the business. To govern and guide the EA team thought process, a proven and flexible architecture methodology like The Open Group Architecture Framework (TOGAF) is needed.

" AM I FAMILAR WITH TOGAF? I MAY BE -
WHAT'S HIS FIRST NAME? "

Copyright © Al Johns, Used with Permission

TOGAF is one of the most widely used Enterprise Architecture methodologies today with an estimated 80 percent of Global 50 companies and 60 percent of Fortune 500 companies utilizing its' methodologies. Global TOGAF 9 Certifications exceed 70,000 in 134 countries. At the high-level, TOGAF is broken down into four (4) architectural domains that offer specializations for businesses.

- **Business architecture:** includes information on business strategy, capabilities and business process flow.
- **Data architecture:** defines the data necessary to support the business architecture, including logical and physical data models that define the system of record, system of reference, integrations, storage, management and maintenance.
- **Applications architecture:** provides a blueprint for structuring and deploying application systems in accordance with business goals, organizational standards and core business processes.

- **Technical architecture:** describes the necessary IT infrastructure and networking involved in developing and supporting business applications. Technical knowledge of cloud architectures patterns, identity and access management, and networking concepts such as firewalls, storage and load-balancing, are all important.

At the heart of TOGAF is the Architecture Development Method (ADM) depicted in Exhibit 1. The ADM is the Enterprise Architecture process lifecycle. What I like about the TOGAF ADM is that it is iterative and flexible. This flexibility is key since it allows your EA practice to support the two operation modes mentioned earlier: Strategic and Tactical.

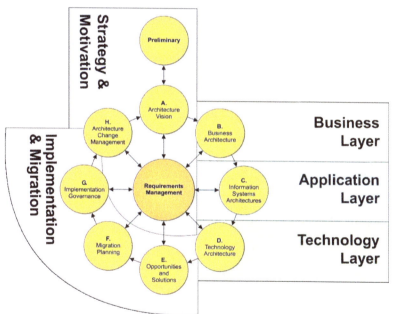

EXHIBIT 1: TOGAF ARCHITECTURE DEVELOPMENT METHOD
Copyright © 2009-2011, The Open Group

11

Strategically, ADM helps businesses assess and overhaul their IT systems in order to support transformation. Transformation, as defined by Merriam-Webster®, is the act or process of changing completely. ADM supports transformation efforts by helping you develop a north star vision mapping requirements, process and technologies into actionable workstreams necessary for business to efficiently compete in today's digitally economies. ADM helps bridge the gap between IT and the business through a common language.

Tactically, you use ADM to streamline project delivery and execution processes so that they can be reproducible with fewer errors. Using TOGAF ADM, you can define and organize project goals and requirements before the project starts; therefore, keeping the process moving with fewer exceptions, staying on time, on budget and aligning IT with business to produce quality results. Proven and real-life experiences for the various TOGAF ADM phases I have been assembled in this book in the following chapters.

- **Preliminary**: Architecture Principles (Chapter 5)
- **Phase A**: Architecture Vision, Viewpoints and Reference Patterns (Chapter 8)
- **Phase B-D**: Architecture Deliverables (Chapter 7)
- **Phase G**: Architecture Engagement (Chapter 6)
- **Phase H**: Architecture Reference Repository (Chapter 9)

What about Security?

Although Security (both information and risk management) is not specifically identified as a TOGAF domain, Security is unique since it cuts across the four (4) TOGAF domains. An important aspect of an architecture is the quality of the information and how it is managed to enable safe, secure, reliable and accurate data, as well as addressing risk areas throughout the company. No longer a by-product of applications or infrastructure, data is a

Merriam-Webster is trademark of Merriam-Webster, Incorporated

prime. As a prime, data by itself is a strategic enabler and competitive differentiator. Security must always be closely associated with the original Enterprise Architecture efforts; trying to add later is costly. This is where TOGAF shines. It provides a common framework and vocabulary to organize and communicate across departmental IT efforts.

****

Take-Away

➢ Key benefits of TOGAF are:
  o Saves time and money by utilizing proven methods to drive best solutions more effectively.
  o Considers the holistic, end-to-end vision based on a common set of artifacts and models so everyone speaks the same language.
  o Based on Enterprise Architecture open methods and global standards.
➢ Since everyone likes to have "Architect" in their title, all Enterprise Architects in your practice need to be TOGAF certified to distinguish themselves from other self-proclaimed "Architects" in the organization.
➢ TOGAF in an extensive framework and can be daunting to implement, but as you will learn in later chapters, you do not have to use every part of TOGAF to be successful. Understanding the basics is adequate for success in Part 2.

****

Chapter 2 - APQC: Your Business Process Framework

I admire people who can successfully grow plants. Unfortunately, plants do not thrive in my care. I did not know you could kill a cactus until I accidently killed one. The only plants that survive in my care are artificial ones, and then I keep a rake handy to sweep up the plastic leaves.

Luckily, living plants have a remarkable self-healing capacity called dedifferentiation that allows their cells and tissues to regenerate after damage and/or injury. Dedifferentiation allows a plant (and some amphibians) to regrow a limb if one is broken off. Despite its apparent distance from biology, Information Technology (IT) has also evolved and shifted towards frameworks that enable a self-healing capability through redundancy and high availability. But, unlike plants, thinking is involved in IT planning and the ability to failover.

But what if the entire business IT organization could 'self-heal' and flex in pace and rhythm of the business to constantly maintain a forefront position as strategic enabler? That would indeed be something to see and get excited about; however, this always sounds like hype and big claims that most executives have learned to be skeptical.

The good news is, this section will lay the foundation for creating the Living Architecture View of your organization's active IT business landscape. To create this view, you are going to utilize another industry framework; you will inventory and catalog enterprise-wide capabilities and business processes. Process frameworks are essentially a list of all the key processes performed in an organization, grouped hierarchically to show how they relate to each other. The hierarchy is important since it provides a complete panoramic picture of your processes and sub-processes. Process frameworks (Exhibit 2) also enable the EA practice to perform Capability Based Planning (CBP), which provides executives with an understanding of what capabilities are missing, are at risk, provide competitive advantages or should be standardized as a commodity (Exhibit 2).

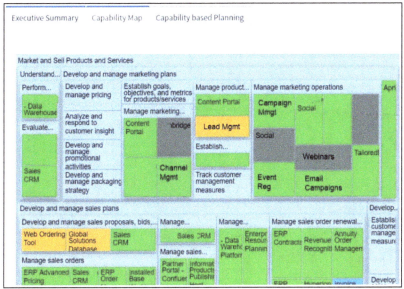

EXHIBIT 2: CAPABILITY MAP WITH SUPPORTING APPLICATIONS

What is the difference between a **Capability** and a **Process**[2]?

- **Capabilities are how work gets done and Processes are what work gets done**. A process is a series of interrelated activities that takes inputs and produces results (outputs).
- **A Capability should be described with a noun; a Process is a verb + noun.** Capabilities are nouns because they represent concepts. Processes are verbs because they perform an action to a concept. For example, "Accounts Payable" is a capability (noun) while "Process accounts payable" is a process (verb +noun).

By stocktaking and assessing your business capabilities, you can start to map the applications and processes; informing the organization on steps, data and sequence (Exhibit 3). While this task might sound daunting, there is no need to be a Pioneer starting from scratch.

EXHIBIT 3: SAMPLE APQC CAPABILITY WITH SUPPORTING BUSINESS PROCESSES

Developed in 1992, APCQ is a popular business Process Classification Framework® (PCF) which has been successfully adopted by hundreds of organizations worldwide. What I like about APQC is it also includes IT capabilities along with HR, Finance, Sales/Marketing, Customer Service, etc. Most agree that IT and Business planning need to converge, with IT underpinning the business. In the Living Architecture View, IT and business need to plan the investment strategy together covering people, process and technology. By using APQC, you do not need to implement other frameworks like COBIT® when one framework, namely APQC, meets both.

Homework Assignment for Chapter 10: Go to the APQC website (https://www.apqc.org) and download the APQC Process Classification

COBIT® is a registered trademark of ISACA and the IT Governance Institute.

Framework Excel file that is suitable for your industry. Since the APQC framework can be detailed, start with the first three (3) levels which are: **Level 1 Category**, **Level 2 Process Group** and **Level 3 Process**. In the downloaded APQC Excel sheet, add a column to assign a business owner for each element. You will revisit this in Part Three.

****

Take-Away

- ➤ APQC saves you time and effort by providing an industry standard process framework as a basis to build and model capabilities and business processes.
- ➤ Repel efforts to incorporate other industry and vendor frameworks in addition to APQC. Incorporating multiple process frameworks adds planning complexity with more (unnecessary) work to merge and manage the combined Capabilities and Business Process names.
- ➤ Having a panoramic picture of all your processes and sub-processes will also accelerate merger and acquisition (M&A) due diligence by providing an accurate mapping of business technologies.

****

Chapter 3 - CMMI Maturity Model: Measure success

To begin this section, let's consider a "joke" we used to tell in the office.

A new CIO [or CEO, CTO, etc..] has been hired to run an IT department. The previous CIO meets with the new CIO privately, and presents three numbered envelopes. "Open these if you run into serious trouble," says the former CIO.

Three months later there is crisis and the new CIO is taking a lot of heat. Beginning to panic, the new CIO remembers the three envelopes and quickly takes out the first. The message reads, "Blame your predecessor." The new CIO quickly reports that the previous CIO had left a real mess and it was taking a lot longer than expected to clean up, but everything was on the right track. Satisfied with the comments, the CIO was allowed to keep the job.

Three months later there is another crisis. Having learned from the previous experience, the new CIO quickly opens the second envelope. The message reads, "Reorganize."; therefore, the new CIO fires key people, consolidates groups and tries to cut costs. The CIO is applauded for swift actions and the CIO keeps the job.

Three more months pass and the organization is still struggling. The CIO goes into his/her office, closes the door, and opens the third envelope. The message says, "Write three envelopes."

Let's face it, C-Suite turnover is at record highs. There is a wealth of research that details how new executives should transition into their leading role; however, many successors who follow a long serving successful executive struggle in the transition. According to industry surveys, the median tenure of C-suite executive is five years, with as little as 2-3 years in public companies. Putting humor aside, if the new CIO in our joke would have relied on Enterprise Architecture and implemented the next topic, he/she would not have been writing envelopes.

Originally developed at Carnegie Mellon University, Capability Maturity Model Integration (CMMI) is an appraisal process model designed to provide a baseline to improve the performance of the existing organizational standards, processes and procedures. CMMI is meant to help organizations (and EA practices) improve their "capability" to consistently and predictably deliver services or products, and NOT to redefine them. CMMI defines the following maturity levels for processes (Exhibit 4).

Characteristics of the Maturity levels

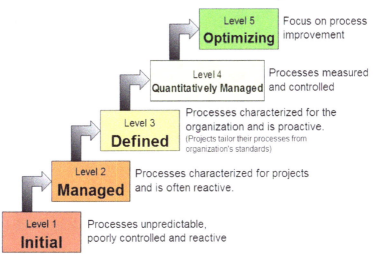

EXHIBIT 4: CMMI MATURITY LEVELS

As an appraisal process model, CMMI can be tuned for different scenarios and can be used to guide process improvement across a project, business unit, or an entire organization. CMMI models provide guidance for developing or improving processes that meet the business goals of an organization. With the focus on Enterprise Architecture operating in both tactical and strategic modes, we have two (2) tuned CMMI models:

1. Tactical CMMI model to measure the EA practice maturity level.
2. Strategic CMMI model to measure the EA value to the organization.

It is important to note that when defined, CMMI maturity levels cannot be skipped. You cannot jump from Level 1 to Level 3 in one swoop, skipping

Level 2. CMMI maturity levels are transformational; therefore, plan to spend a year moving from one level to the next. With that said, the goal of this book is to jumpstart your EA practice and career by getting you to Level 3/4 maturity as soon as possible!

Tactical

Tactical refers to those activities that can be measured within the EA practice with minimal reliance on other teams. These activities are process improvement programs within EA's control. In fact, many people would argue these activities are part of the EA mission; therefore, the tactical EA CMMI model (Exhibit 5) focuses on EA process improvement programs that will help reach the optimized Living Architecture view faster.

Tactical / Strategic	Maturity Level / Area	Level 1 Initial	Level 2 Managed	Level 3 Defined	Level 4 Quantitively Managed	Level 5 Optimizing
Tactical — Architecture Engagement	Architecture Adoption	Lack of formal EA practice but there maybe pockets of "Architects".	EA Practice with defined Methodology, but lack the support across the entire enterprise. EA team reactive to crisis.	Architecture Principles documented. Architecture imbedded in PMO Processes.	EA Practice established and understood across the enterprise. Enterprise Architects TOGAF certified. CMMI metrics reported to C-Level	EA organization recognized contributor to company strategic vision and roadmaps. Living Architecture is a reality
	Architecture Governance	EA oversight non-existent. Shadow IT and technical debt pervasive across enterprise.	Minimal EA oversight. Shadow IT and technical debt still pervasive but recognized in prohibiting growth.	Architecture methods formalized and projects tailored to include Architecture. SDOs, Whiteboards, Assessments, Pilots, POCs in practice.	Measured success in reducing shadow IT and technical debt across enterprise. Implementations of NODs, Viewpoints, reference architectures and ARB review board.	EA governance processes being perfected and tuned. EA tool used to model and visually depicts the Living Architecture.
	Business Process Architecture	Business processes not formally document across enterprise.	General understanding to inventory critical processes and owners, but limited understanding of cross-functional dependencies.	APQC being used to proactively inventory capabilities, processes and owners.	Business capability planning a reality with all processes inventoried, documented and their lifecycles denoted..	Alignment with Living Architecture to produce 'what if' scenarios and guide strategic direction.
	Data/Information Architecture	Data oversight non-existent. Data silos and duplicate data pervasive across enterprise.	Minimal EA oversight, but recognition data quality critical for growth. Basic inventory of core data objects and owners (often in Excel)	Formal inventory of data objects, owners and relation to process. Data governance in place and aspirations for master data management (MDM)	MDM implemented along with reference patterns to publish data between system or record and system of reference.	Data objects and dependencies modeled in EA tool. Ability to perform 'what if' scenarios aligned with Living Architecture.
	Applications Architecture	Application oversight non-existent. Shadow IT and duplicate applications pervasive across enterprise.	Minimal EA oversight, but recognition duplicative applications increasing cost and impacting growth. Basic inventory of applications and owners (often in Excel)	Formal inventory of applications, owners, lifecycles and relation to process. Application governance in place.	Application contracts and renewal dates tracked.	Applications mapped to capabilities and processes EA tool. Ability to model costs and 'what if' scenarios aligned with Living Architecture.
	Infrastructure Architecture	EA oversight non-existent. Shadow IT and technical debt pervasive across enterprise.	Minimal EA oversight. Shadow IT and technical debt still pervasive but recognized as significant risk to company due to Security threats and outages.	Initial inventory of infrastructure and lifecycles. Infrastructure/Security governance in place.	Formal automated inventory of infrastructure assets (physical assets, OS, network) in place. Projects automatically kick-off to remediate anything n-1	Full infrastructure compliance and modeled to the Living Architecture.

EXHIBIT 5: CMMI MATURITY LEVEL DESCRIPTIONS (TACTICAL)

- **Architecture Adoption-** In order for the EA program to be effective it must be incorporated across the organization and reflect the strategic planning horizon. To tactically accomplish Level 3 maturity, EA must adopt:

- A methodology (TOGAF) that is both flexible and scalable to business change.
- Architecture Principles to influence good IT behavior to prevent shadow IT and siloed data.

The work does not stop there. Both TOGAF and Architecture Principles must be executed in a way that is recognized by the entire company. To accomplish this and get to the next maturity level, leading Architecture programs devote considerable efforts ensuring key Architecture stakeholders understand and support the program and constantly communicate the business benefits.

- **Enterprise Architecture Governance-** Successful EA governance is a cultural orientation defining a set of responsibilities to ensure an organization's IT architectural integrity and effectiveness. An important maturity indicator for successful EA programs is a high degree of business involvement in both the creation and enforcement of the EA governance processes which has been incorporated across the organization. With mature EA programs, understanding of concepts and appreciation for EA materials like solution designs, whiteboard sessions, architecture assessments, Pilots, POCs, NODs become synonymous with good IT behavior and start the natural progression to a target state architecture. Although notionally you can track EA Governance by sentiment, tracking the following elements provides tactical insights into EA adoption and success.
  - Projects requested by the business (in the project pipeline queue) waiting for approval vs approved projects per month (utilization)
  - Active Projects w/ an Architect vs Active Projects w/out an Architect

- Projects at risk w/ an Architect vs Projects at risk w/out an Architect
- # Notice of Decision (NODs) completed
- # Assessments completed
- # Solution Design Documents (SDDs) completed
- # Pilots/Proof-of-Concepts (POCs) completed

- **Business Process Architecture (BPA)-** The BPA reflects the expression of the company's key business strategies and their impact on core business processes. Mature EA programs typically consist of 'As-Is' and 'To-Be' models of the business organization, functions, and core processes. By implementing APQC, you can quickly demonstrate Level 3 maturity by showing that the business capabilities and processes have been defined and inventoried. Level 4 maturity represents the Living Enterprise Architecture View, and requires documenting the business processes and capabilities in a tool for better understanding and analysis. A Level 4 EA practice can quickly:
  - Display 'As-Is' business processes with opportunities for improvement.
  - Provide 'What-If' scenarios to analyze business impact and improve business decision making.
  - Categorize process lifecycles as either commodities (low change), strategic (ROI differentiation) or new investments (innovation) to assist in investment decisions.

  Rigorously applied, documenting the BPA enables the EA team to apprise corporate decision-making in a number of areas leading to a multitude of benefits.

- **Information/ Data Architecture (DA) -** DA is a business architecture driven set of models that express data and analytic capabilities. The DA represents a strategic asset that must be pervasive throughout the business value chain to improve processes, decision-making and a sustainable competitive advantage. Accurate information is essential to the quality and efficiency of decision-making. A Level 3 organization will have a formal inventory of data objects, owners and their relation to the business processes. Data governance enables data owners and stewards to agree on data definitions and propose metadata changes without impacting the entire company. For example, is a Sales Account the same as an ERP Account?

Although notionally you can track Information Architecture by sentiment, mature EA practices also track the following to gain tactical insights of adoption and success.

- o # core data objects
- o # data owners
- o # integrations w/ core data objects
- o # databases / tables / views / users / queries

- **Applications/ Solutions Architecture-** The Application Architecture proactively involves the EA team with Application Portfolio Management (APM). APM is the formal inventory of information systems needed to satisfy business needs. Level 3 programs incorporate the business, information, and technology requirements in managing the application portfolio by identifying applications, their owners, lifecycles, costs/contracts and relationships to business process and infrastructure. Leading EA practices take this a step further by incorporating metrics like system performance and incidents to help answer questions, such as:

  - o Finance:
    - ▪ Which departments have the most application spend?
    - ▪ What is the actual cost of an application?
    - ▪ What is the distribution of budget?
    - ▪ Are we investing according to strategy?

- Performance/Security:
  - Which applications have the most incidents?
  - What applications are on old versions of hardware/software and represent business vulnerabilities? (e.g. Greater than two versions behind)
  - What are the hardware/software counts?
- Strategy:
  - What applications can be moved to the cloud vs on-premise?
  - What is the organizational impact of moving an application?

- **Technology Architecture-** The Technology Architecture consists of a set of standards and models that guide engineering decisions for information systems and technology infrastructure. Common, shared applications and infrastructure across the organization is strongly preferred over the deployment of numerous duplicate IT investments with limited utility outside a particular business unit or function. Level 3 EA programs use the inventories gathered in the BPA, DA and APM to identify linkages and ensure the evolution of an adaptive infrastructure. By appraising the IT portfolio in a manner that places priority on common systems, standardization of data and processes, greater opportunities exist for information collaboration, process efficiency, and cost control.

Strategic

Strategically, companies want to maximize growth by producing quality products and services, while reducing costs. The strategic EA CMMI model (Exhibit 6) focuses on using industry benchmarks to measure positive impact. The rationale is to show executive leadership that EA is in fact moving the needle by making contributions to organizational value and business competitiveness.

Tactical / Strategic	Maturity Level / Area	Level 1 Initial	Level 2 Managed	Level 3 Defined	Level 4 Quantitively Managed	Level 5 Optimizing
Strategic Architecture Impact to Organization	Cost of IT	IT costs poorly tracked	IT budget defined but not comprehensive due to pervasive shadow IT and technical debt.	Industry IT benchmark costs understand. Tracking and measurement of IT costs to those benchmarks	IT Costs controlled and benchmark targets met.	Focus on being a leader for industry benchmarks. Living Architecture is recognized as a discriminating factor.
	Quality	Enterprise quality processes poorly controlled and reactive.	Initial EA oversight. Quality issues recognized as prohibiting growth; however, initiatives are reactive.	Architecture methods formalized and adopted to improve quality. Includes SDDs, Whiteboards, Assessments.	Measured success in improving quality across enterprise. Implementations Viewpoints and reference architectures to improve quality.	EA governance processes being perfected and tuned. EA tool used to model and visually depicts the Living Architecture.
	Net Promoter Score (NPS)	NPS not tracked	NPS defined but not understood.	NPS understood and compared to peers and industry benchmarks. NPS goals defined.	NPS targets met.	Focus on leading peers and industry benchmarks in NPS scores. Living Architecture is recognized as a discriminating factor.

EXHIBIT 6: CMMI MATURITY LEVEL DESCRIPTIONS (STRATEGIC)

- **Cost of IT** – Comparing IT spending as a percentage of company revenue is a common method to calculate the Cost of IT. The method is straightforward, divide total IT budget by the company's total revenue, or number of employees, or number of desktops supported.

Although covered in more detail in Chapter 12, using a reputable IT Benchmark survey for cost comparisons in a useful technique. For example, let's say you are a high-tech company and you want to compare your IT desktop/laptop spend as a percentage of IT budget. If surveyed companies spend $5K - $10K per desktop, then you can plot your current spend with established executive leadership goals.

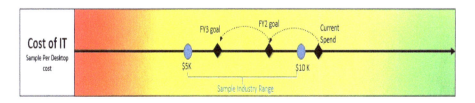

- **Quality Assurance-** Quality Assurance efforts usually fall on the product development side of the organization. Product development usually operates with their own 'architects', standards and practices since, by their nature, they are the technical experts for innovation and profits. However, there are areas of IT reliance used by the business to

25

meet business goals whose data quality is paramount. Having a TOGAF-based architecture discipline at the table with a proven and meaningful materials such as SDD templates, facilitated whiteboard sessions, assessment processes and implementations of Viewpoints and reference architectures improves the business quality. Examples are:

- o Product questions:
  - Do we know what customers need?
  - Do we have the right product portfolio?
    Quality Issue: Data accuracy in Order Entry and Inventory management systems.

- o Sales questions:
  - Can we convert prospects to customers?
  - Is our Sales Forecast accurate?
  - Is our sales planning effective?
    Quality Issue: Data accuracy and consistency across Sales, ERP, Marketing and campaign management systems.

- o Customer Retention questions:
  - Are we net gaining/losing customers?
  - What is our customer churn?
  - Do we deliver as promised?
    Quality Issue: Data accuracy and consistency across customer health (telemetry data), Sales and Service Management systems.

- **NPS -** Net Promoter Score (NPS) is a very common and important customer experience metric used by companies to engage and measure customer sentiment. NPS scores usually boil down to a number between 1-100 with 100 being outstanding. Because NPS is so important, NPS scores can be found for most industries as well as your competition. With NPS you can:

- o Segment customers by loyalty
- o Identify unsatisfied and at-risk customers
- o Optimize around a single customer metric
- o Benchmark against industry and competitor scores
- o Uncover customer loyalty drivers
- o Monitor improvements in products, services and across the entire customer journey

By way of example, let's say your peer industry NPS range is between 75 to 90. Based on your own customer surveys, your NPS score is approximately 60. Working with executive leadership, you can set new improvement targets for future years.

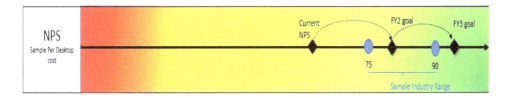

****

Take-Away

- ➢ Implementing a CMMI maturity model shows that architecture has a strategic vision and eye on continued improvement and transformation.
- ➢ Visibly display and track EA maturity models in the EA Repository (Chapter 9).

****

Chapter 4 –EVM: Data Driven Project Status and Health

Although Earned Value Management (EVM) is typically associated with Finance or the Project Management Office (PMO), and not Enterprise Architecture, it is an important topic for EAs to understand since it uses data to quantify and predict project status and health. Without EVM, project status reports are based on sentiment. EVM removes the sentiment and provides an objective project health "early warning signal". In the Living Architecture View, objectivity is critical since you want data to guide decisions and help us proactively manage project risks while the project budget remains intact.

EVM is a project management technique for measuring project performance and progress so you can notice warning signs and intervene immediately. If you have ever worked on a project where project status can go from "Green" to "Yellow" to "Red" based on the Project Manager (PM) setting a color, understanding core concepts in EVM is worthwhile. In simple terms, EVM tracks budgeted vs actuals in costs and work to statistically predict final project Cost at Completion (CAC) and expected delivery times. Without EVM, project status can be left to the control and state of mind of the PMO. By human nature, no one wants to report their projects being "Red" or "Yellow"; therefore, the PM will often report "Green" even if Divine intervention is required.

"...and I think we all know who is responsible for the spectacular turnaround in the Finance Project."
("The Wizard", n.d.)

28

My interest in EVM came from my first programming job after college. I was hired as an entry level software developer by a company that recently had won a large contract. Because this was a new business opportunity for the company, they bid low and then staffed it with junior level talent. Not surprisingly, the early contract phases did not go well. As new college hires, we did not have the discipline to draft solution design documents or the organizational skills to schedule cross-functional whiteboard sessions. As you can guess, the project quickly went from "Green" to "Yellow" to "Red". New PMs were brought in to get the project on track as well as senior contractors, at premium rates, to augment us junior staffers. A couple years late and over budget, the project was finally delivered. As an outcome, all of us still standing were sent to learn EVM and project planning concepts. The course made an impact on me and I still keep my pocket reference guide today.

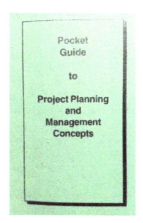

A common complaint about EVM is the time and resources necessary to implement it. This is a fair objection, because detailed EVM is traditionally implemented by large organizations with mature Finance departments and Project Controllers who specialize in EVM. These individuals work with the PMs to intake weekly project status and compare project actuals in costs, work complete and schedule to uncover variances and identify critical paths.

However, there is a minimal version of EVM that architects should know and promote to quantify project performance and progress. The fantastic part about the simplified version is it relies on data that PMs should be already be tracking: budget, schedule and tasks.

The simplified version of EVM involves ten (10) data points shown in Table 1, but six (6) of those data points are calculated based on actual values entered for budget, costs and value earned. The green row is entered at project start. The blue rows are calculated values and variances during each project phase, and the yellow rows are calculated indices and estimates.

TABLE 1: EVM TERMS

Term	Definition	Determined	Formula
Budget at Completion (BAC)	BAC is the total estimated budget to complete the entire project for a given schedule. (Labor, Materials, Licenses, etc.)	Determined at project start.	N/A
Planned Value (PV)	PV is the term to describe the estimated amount of money that was budgeted to completed a certain task by a certain date.	Determined at project start by estimating the work value in each project phase.	N/A
Earned Value (EV)	EV represents the estimated value earned by completing work. For example, if your project is 10 sprints, then EV for each sprint can be BAC/10 (simple estimation).	Tracked and entered during Project execution.	EV = BAC x % Work Complete
Actual Cost (AC)	AC is the actual amount of PV; it describes the amount of money that was actually spent to get a certain task done by a certain time.	Tracked and entered during Project execution.	

Schedule Variance (SV)	SV shows the difference between how long work took versus what you planned related to money being spent.	Calculated	$SV = EV - PV$
Cost Variance (CV)	CV shows the difference between the amount of value that you earned on a task (EV) and the actual cost (AC) that was performed.	Calculated	$CV = EV - AC$
Schedule Performance Index (SPI)	SPI provides an instantaneous check on schedule at any point in the project. SPI < 1 means you are behind schedule – you are not earning the value on the timeline you planned.	Calculated SPI < 1 is poor.	$SPI = EV/PV$
Cost Performance Index (CPI)	CPI provides an instantaneous check on cost at any point in the project. CPI < 1 means you are behind in cost – you are spending more than you are earning on the timeline you planned.	Calculated CPI < 1 is poor	$CPI = EV/AC$
Estimate at Completion (EAC)	EAC is a handy number to know because it predicts your final project costs at project complete anytime during the project.	Calculated	$EAC = BAC / CPI$
Estimate to Complete (ETC)	ETC is also a handy number to know because it predicts how much budget you will need to complete the project at any time during the project.	Calculated	$ETC = EAC - AC$

EVM Example – The bathroom remodel.

To understand the simplified version of EVM, let's say you plan to have a bathroom remodeled. The contractor estimates it will take four (4) weeks and cost $7800. The EVM Project Plan is:

- Budget at Completion (BAC) is $7800 ($5000 labor and $2800 in materials)
    - Sheetrock/drywall = $600
    - New Shower/tub = $1000
    - New toilet = $400
    - New sink/vanity = $500
    - New mirror and light fixtures = $300
    - Labor budget is $5000
        - Electrician = 1 day $800
        - Plumber = 1 day $1200
        - Miscellaneous Labor $30/hour. Plan for 25 hours per week $3000

- The four (4) week project schedule is based on the following estimates (Table 2).
    - **Week 1** = Demolish old bathroom and install new sheetrock
        EV = ($7800) BAC * .25 (25% complete) = $1950
        PV = Sheetrock + labor ($750) = $1350
    - **Week 2** = Install new shower, toilet and new sink
        EV = ($7800) BAC * .5 (50% complete) = $3900
        PV = prior week PV + shower/toilet/sink + plumber ($1200) + labor ($750) = $5200
    - **Week 3** = Install light fixture and paint.
        EV = ($7800) BAC * .75 (75% complete) = $5850
        PV = prior week PV + fixtures ($300) + Electrician ($800) + labor ($750) = $7050
    - **Week 4** = Touch-up and project complete
        EV = ($7800) BAC * 1 (100% complete) = $7800
        PV = prior week PV + labor ($750) = $7800

Table 2 represents the expected project budget, schedule and costs at project start.

TABLE 2: EVM PROJECT START

	Start	Week 1	Week 2	Week 3	Week 4
Budget at Completion	$7,800				
Earned Value (EV)	$0	$1,950	$3,900	$5,850	$7,800
Planned Value (PV)		$1,350	$5,200	$7,050	$7,800
Actual Costs (AC)	$0	$0	$0	$0	$0
Schedule Variance (SV)		$0	$0	$0	$0
Cost Variance (CV)		$0	$0	$0	$0
Schedule Performance Index (SPI)		--	--	--	--
Cost Performance Index (CPI)		--	--	--	--
Estimate at Complete (EAC)	$0	$0	$0	$0	
Estimate to Complete (ETC)	$0	$0	$0	$0	

Week 1: Contractor arrives on time. Bathroom demolished and new sheetrock/drywall installed. Contractor needed to spend an extra $200 to rent a truck to haul debris away. Total labor hours were 30 hours. Contractor reports everything on schedule.

- Actual Cost (AC) = $600 + $200 + $900 = $1700
- Schedule Variance (SV) = $1950 (EV) - $1350 (PV) = $600 ahead of schedule
- Cost Variance (CV) = $1950 (EV) – $1700 (AC) = $250 ahead of budget
- SPI = 1.44 = Ahead on performance
- CPI = 1.15 = Ahead on cost

TABLE 3: EVM PROJECT WEEK #1

	Start	Week 1	Week 2	Week 3	Week 4
Budget at Completion	$7,800				
Earned Value (EV)	$0	$1,950	$3,900	$5,850	$7,800
Planned Value (PV)		$1,350	$5,200	$7,050	$7,800
Actual Costs (AC)		$1,700	$5,600	$7,450	$8,050

Schedule Variance (SV)	$600	$0	$0	$0
Cost Variance (CV)	$250	$0	$0	$0
Schedule Performance Index (SPI)	1.44	$0	$0	$0
Cost Performance Index (CPI)	1.15	--	--	--
Estimate at Complete (EAC)	$6,800.00	--	--	--
Estimate to Complete (ETC)	$5,100.00	$0	$0	$0

Week 2: Plumber arrives to install shower, toilet and new sink. Unfortunately, the sink is late. Plumber had to come back the next day for 4 hours to install sink costing an extra $500. Miscellaneous labor was 10 hours. Contractor reports everything on schedule.

- Actual Cost (AC) = prior week AC + shower/toilet/sink + plumber ($1700) + labor ($300) = $5600
- Schedule Variance (SV) = $3900 (EV) - $5200 (PV) = ($1300) behind schedule
- Cost Variance (CV) = $3900 (EV) – $5600 (AC) = ($1700) over budget
- SPI = .75 = Behind on performance
- CPI = .70 = Behind on cost

TABLE 4: EVM PROJECT WEEK #2

	Start	Week 1	Week 2	Week 3	Week 4
Budget at Completion	$7,800				
Earned Value (EV)	$0	$1,950	$3,900	$5,850	$7,800
Planned Value (PV)		$1,350	$5,200	$7,050	$7,800
Actual Costs (AC)		$1,700	$5,600	$7,450	$8,050
Schedule Variance (SV)		$600	($1,300)	$0	$0
Cost Variance (CV)		$250	($1,700)	$0	$0
Schedule Performance Index (SPI)		1.44	0.75	$0	$0
Cost Performance Index (CPI)		1.15	0.70	--	--
Estimate at Complete (EAC)		$6,800.00	$11,200.00	--	--
Estimate to Complete (ETC)		$5,100.00	$5,600.00	$0	$0

34

Week 3: Electrician arrives to install light fixtures and completes job in 4 hours. Bathroom painting starts and completes. Saved $400 on electrician but spent extra $400 for paint and supplies. Miscellaneous labor was 30 hours. Contractor reports everything on schedule.

- Actual Cost (AC) = prior week AC + fixtures ($300) + Electrician ($400) + supplies ($400) + labor ($750) = $7450
- Schedule Variance (SV) = $5850 (EV) - $7050 (PV) = ($1200) behind schedule
- Cost Variance (CV) = $5850 (EV) – $7450 (AC) = ($1600) over budget
- SPI = .83 = Still behind on performance but improving
- CPI = .79 = Still behind on cost but improving

TABLE 5: EVM PROJECT WEEK #3

	Start	Week 1	Week 2	Week 3	Week 4
Budget at Completion	$7,800				
Earned Value (EV)	$0	$1,950	$3,900	$5,850	$7,800
Planned Value (PV)		$1,350	$5,200	$7,050	$7,800
Actual Costs (AC)		$1,700	$5,600	$7,450	$8,050
Schedule Variance (SV)		$600	($1,300)	($1,200)	$0
Cost Variance (CV)		$250	($1,700)	($1,600)	$0
Schedule Performance Index (SPI)		1.44	0.75	0.83	$0
Cost Performance Index (CPI)		1.15	0.70	0.79	--
Estimate at Complete (EAC)		$6,800.00	$11,200.00	$9,933.33	--
Estimate to Complete (ETC)		$5,100.00	$5,600.00	$2,483.33	$0

Week 4: Final touch-ups. Project complete and signed-off. Miscellaneous labor was 20 hours.

- Actual Cost (AC) = prior week AC + labor ($600) = $8050
- Schedule Variance (SV) = $7800 (EV) - $7800 (PV) = $0 on schedule
- Cost Variance (CV) = $7800 (EV) – $8050 (AC) = ($250) over budget
- SPI = 1 = On schedule

- CPI = .97 = Slightly behind on cost; i.e. over budget

TABLE 6: EVM PROJECT WEEK #4

	Start	Week 1	Week 2	Week 3	Week 4
Budget at Completion	$7,800				
Earned Value (EV)	$0	$1,950	$3,900	$5,850	$7,800
Planned Value (PV)		$1,350	$5,200	$7,050	$7,800
Actual Costs (AC)		$1,700	$5,600	$7,450	$8,050
Schedule Variance (SV)		$600	($1,300)	($1,200)	$0
Cost Variance (CV)		$250	($1,700)	($1,600)	($250)
Schedule Performance Index (SPI)		1.44	0.75	0.83	1.00
Cost Performance Index (CPI)		1.15	0.70	0.79	0.97
Estimate at Complete (EAC)		$6,800.00	$11,200.00	$9,933.33	$8,050.00
Estimate to Complete (ETC)		$5,100.00	$5,600.00	$2,483.33	$0.00

Summary: Overall a successful project completing on time and only slight over budget. Week #2 was a pivotal, although the contractor reported everything was on schedule, cost and schedule variances told a different story. After week #2, the EAC was predicting final costs of $11,200 or $1700 over budget. This was the early warning signal that the project may slip.

Luckily week #3 went very well with the electrician and the cost/schedule variances started to shorten. Week #3 went so well, that there was little work needed in week #4 to close out the project. Your contractor was right.

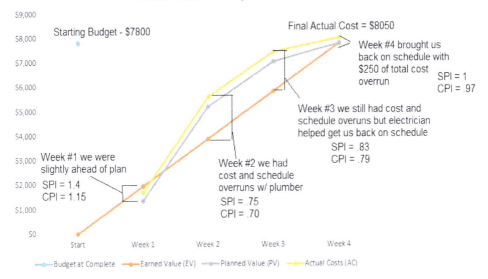

Bathroom Remodel Project

Starting Budget - $7800

Final Actual Cost = $8050

Week #4 brought us back on schedule with $250 of total cost overrun
SPI = 1
CPI = .97

Week #3 we still had cost and schedule overruns but electrician helped get us back on schedule
SPI = .83
CPI = .79

Week #1 we were slightly ahead of plan
SPI = 1.4
CPI = 1.15

Week #2 we had cost and schedule overruns w/ plumber
SPI = .75
CPI = .70

Start   Week 1   Week 2   Week 3   Week 4

Budget at Complete — Earned Value (EV) — Planned Value (PV) — Actual Costs (AC)

****

Take-Away

- ➢ EVM provides early warning signals on project cost and performance; therefore, allowing steps to be taken to correct project execution while the budget is still intact.
- ➢ The simplified version of EVM relies on data that PMs should already be tracking: project budget, schedule and tasks.

****

PART TWO – Tactical Deliverables and Techniques

Welcome to Part 2. In this section you will learn the hands-on techniques and EA deliverables that will provide immediate advancement. In Part 1, you learned about the frameworks required to create a successful Enterprise Architecture (EA) practice. These frameworks establish, build and scale your EA practice and IT.

- TOGAF to establish the Architecture Methodology.
- APQC to inventory and define industry standard business processes and capabilities.
- CMMI Maturity Model to measure EA performance and success.
- EVM to predict project health, schedule and cost.

In this section we will tactically define and construct the deliverables based on these frameworks that are necessary to make decisions, analyze outcomes and present findings. The goal is to drive immediate EA value to the organization and boost your career.

Chapter 5 – Architecture Principles: Good IT Decision Making

In Part 1 you adopted TOGAF as your Architecture methodology. One of my favorite sections in the TOGAF specification[4] is defining **Architecture Principles**. Architecture Principles are like lighthouses on ocean cliffs. Picturesque when the sun is out, but when heavy fog and darkness sets in, their true purpose is revealed by providing a clear reference point for avoiding danger.

Architecture Principles define how the company will leverage and implement IT capabilities and assets to meet business objectives. They represent the core set of rules and best practices that effect a wide range of IT considerations and decisions relevant to aligning technology to business operations. When organizations operate without a set of Architecture Principles, IT short-cuts and convenient exceptions start to erode the technology landscape as departments select solution alternatives to achieve their own goals. These short-term considerations and inconsistencies rapidly undermine the entire IT Architecture resulting in technical debt, overlapping functionality and siloed applications. The unwelcomed outcome from reduced standardization is increased license, infrastructure and support cost. Architecture Principles provide the remedy so companies can make clear and deliberate information technology decisions.

As shown in Exhibit 7, Architecture Principles should be defined in a three (3) level hierarchy. In the hierarchy, Enterprise Principles inform and elaborate IT Principles; and Domain Principles are likewise aligned to the principles at the two higher levels.

> **Enterprise Principles:** High-level corporate values and strategic imperatives that provide a framework to help guide the organization in information technology decisions by aligning business strategies and processes to IT strategy and capabilities.

> **Information Technology (IT) Principles:** IT values and rules that support the Enterprise Principles. These provide the core tenants how technology with be used to make the information environment as productive and cost-effective as possible.

> **Domain Principles:** Values, rules and best practices specific to detailed Architecture domains (e.g., Business, Data, applications, Infrastructure). These establish the detailed specifications for designing and developing information systems that preserve the overall spirit of the Enterprise and IT Principles above them. Domain principles are developed within specific domains to clarify technical standards and usage patterns.

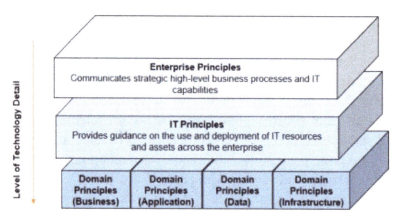

EXHIBIT 7: ENTERPRISE, IT AND DOMAIN PRINCIPLES HIERARCHY

Although principles can come across like universally agreed philosophies such as love your family and respect other' property, just defining principles does not mean that they will be followed or influence good IT behavior. Using the hierarchy above, principles must connect and build on each other. Collectively, these principles are applied as a cohesive set to guide the definition and development of Architecture recommendations and technology decisions. Principles are intended to be long lasting, transforming over time only in response to material changes in the business strategic goals or fundamental technology changes. A quality set of principles are expressed in terms that the business personnel understand and conveys attributes associated with simplicity, relevance, completeness, consistency and stability. IT leadership and key business stakeholder alignment and support for Architecture principles ensure full adoption across relevant IT governance and execution activities.

How to develop Architecture Principles?

A good starting point is your company's annual report which should highlight important strategic pillars for business, security and people/culture. Companies also publish their values on the Internet which can provide inspiration. Ultimately, principles need to be tailored to your organization so they provide relevance and long-lasting guidance for a desired future state. As shown in Exhibit 8, a documented Architecture principle requires an easy to remember Name, Statement, Rationale and Implications.

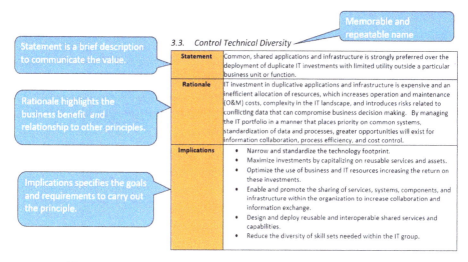

EXHIBIT 8: SAMPLE ENTERPRISE ARCHITECTURE PRINCIPLE

Example: Reuse Before Buy; Buy Before Build

A common architecture principle is "Reuse Before Buy; Buy Before Build". The spirit of this principle is to standardize and maximize existing technology investments and reuse before buying something new. Buying new expands the technology portfolio and often creates duplicate functionality, data inconsistencies and additional license/support costs. By advocating reuse of existing services and assets, you minimize technical debt. If there is not an existing product, then you want to purchase commercial off the shelf products and out-of-the-box (OOTB) solutions before building custom solutions. Custom solutions must be weighed against providing competitive advantage and business value, versus cost to maintain, risks, interoperability and complexity reflected in the IT landscape.

	Build New - Customized	**Out-of-the-Box (OOTB)**
DESIGN APPROACH:	What do you want? 	Will this work? 
TYPICAL BEHAVIOR:	· Starts with the presumption of customization · Significant time spent building common vocabulary about current state process flows – most staff are not good at abstract thinking · Blank white boards cause the group freeze and/or "nice to have wish list" piling on	· Starts with the presumption that OOTB processes will work 80+% of the time · No time spent overcoming group freeze and common vocabulary · Time spent focusing on the true gaps (< 20%) requiring customization · Prevents "nice to have wish list" requirement creep
OUTCOME:	· Difficult "up hill" climb to achieve any benefit from simplification leveraging OOTB	Easy "down hill" movement, when required, to gain benefit from customization

EXHIBIT 9: REUSE BEFORE BUY; BUY BEFORE BUILD PRINCIPLE

****

Take-Away

➢ As a rule of thumb, define approximately ten (10) Enterprise Principles with ten (10) IT Architecture Principles.

➢ Plan to spend two (2) months vetting Principles with key stakeholders to get input and buy-in.

➢ Consistently apply Architecture Principles in assessments and solutions designs to ensure awareness that the IT and business strategies are aligned. Over time you will find that Principles create a cultural shift and natural progression of good IT behavior.

****

Chapter 6 – Implementation: Engagement and Governance

Most will agree that EA provides maximum value at the onset of a project or strategic initiative. If you refer back to the TOGAF ADM, engaging EA during the Preliminary and Architecture Vision phases allows a clear understanding of business goals and drivers to generate the end state architecture product. With the goal of speeding delivery execution, obtaining stakeholder agreement on objectives at project initiation is a critical enabler to attaining desired business outcomes.

However, many projects and business activities start without Architecture involvement. Architecture is brought in after-the-fact to validate a business purchased technology, or when a project is already behind schedule and over budget. The goal of this section is to provide a winning formula for Architecture engagement and project success at project conceptualization by partnering and collaborating with the Program Management Office (PMO).

PMO and the IT Review Board:

I am assuming your company is like most organizations with a defined Program Management Office (PMO) responsible for the structure, planning and management of projects. Whether your company is agile with DevOps or traditional waterfall methodology, a PMO provides project structure by funneling business unit demands and customer priorities into actionable requests which can then be assigned work streams and delivered. The slow death of an IT department occurs when unmanaged, unplanned work is allowed to proceed as shadow IT. You will win when you block unapproved projects and meaningless work from infiltrating the IT system, and you will win more when you can take meaningless work and unplanned projects out of the IT system.

As shown in Exhibit 10, every organization has a funnel process to receive project proposals during the annual planning cycle as well as outside of the annual planning cycle. For purposes of this book, I am defining the **IT Review**

Board as the senior group responsible for reviewing, ranking and sequencing IT work requests. Individuals in this group partner with the business to prioritize their strategic initiatives during the annual planning cycle, as well as disposition ad-hoc proposals. To be effective and move at the speed of business, this group must meet weekly to approve or reject all work requests so the business can obtain answers quickly. Architecture is of course a member of the IT Review Board along with the PMO.

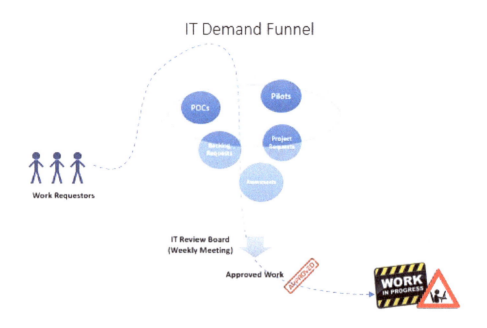

EXHIBIT 10: IT DEMAND FUNNEL

Demand Types:

In my experience, all IT work can be broken down into the six (6) categories that EA is uniquely able to influence. Many IT Review Board meetings get bogged down and derailed with lengthy discussions and confusion of what work is being requested. You cannot let this happen since it wastes time. By categorizing work into these buckets, you can quickly move forward.

1. **Projects***: In the context of this book, a project is defined as any work request that requires more than one-month level of effort (LOE), cross-functional support and/or third party spend. A PM and an Architect must be assigned at the IT Review Board when the project is approved and before the project can proceed. Projects official start with a PM provided **Project Kickoff Deck.** After the kickoff, the Architecture will create a TOGAF inspired Solution Design Document (SDD) for review and approval.

2. **Backlog***: Unlike a project, if the work request requires less than one-month LOE and can be isolated to a specific team, then this work should be assigned to that team's backlog. An architect does not need to be assigned since there is no fundamental change to the IT Landscape. The IT Review Board can close out this work request.

3. **Assessments**: In the spirit of keeping the IT Review Board meeting moving fast and efficient, assessments are useful when there needs to be a better understanding and/or guidance on a topic before a formal work decision can be made. By EA raising its hand and offering to do these assessments helps promote the role of being a technology thought leader. Assessments can be categorized two (2) ways:
   a. **Quick Assessments** generally take less than eight (8) hours to complete and used when architecture/IT needs to quickly weigh-in on pros/cons for a given approach. The deliverable is a PowerPoint deck with an evaluation matrix qualifying the recommendation over five (5) criteria: Cost, Architecture Fit, Business Fit, Quality, Security/Risk. All criteria maintain the same 20% weight for scoring.
   b. **Detailed Assessments** generally take a minimum of six (6) weeks and are run as a project with an assigned PM and core team members who provide assessment requirements and score solutions. Detailed assessments involve coordination with multiple vendors for demos and scoring functionality by

core team members. The assessment deliverable is detailed document from the architect capturing requirements, demos and scoring to arrive at a recommended solution over the same five (5) criteria. Criterion might have different weights, e.g. Security/Risk might be weighted higher than Cost.

4. **Proof of Concept (POC)**: As the name implies, POCs are small efforts led by a certain team to demonstrate feasibility of a solution and/or product; however, there is no path to production. Once the POC is complete, the team must uninstall the solution /product from the IT Landscape. POCs are useful for teams to demo solutions as close to real-life as possible. For example, POCs provide transparency for the infrastructure team to test network equipment on the corporate environment with full awareness. POCs should be time bound less than 90 days with the team reporting back the POC results. With a POC, a PM and/or architect assigned is optional.

5. **Pilot**: Pilots are similar to a POC; however, a successful Pilot can proceed to production. To qualify for success, a Pilot must be accompanied by a **Pilot Charter** that identifies the pilot's objectives and approximately 5-10 success criteria to measure outcomes. Pilots are useful for teams to "try before buy" a solution, or in the initial phase of an enterprise rollout to work out obstacles. Pilots should also be time bound to less than 90 days with the team reporting back the Pilot Charter results for final decision. Best practice is to assign a PM and an architect to a Pilot to make sure objectives, timeframes and success criteria are maintained.

6. **Notice of Decision (NOD)**: A **NOD** is designed to fill the gap in the Demand process by allowing a formal request method for changes and/or exceptions to IT standards. A NOD is a notification, not a solution, and secures a high-level understanding of business need, approach, funding and level of impact to IT, Procurement and Security.

NODs help reduce technical debt by providing transparency and justification for business requests that may overlap with existing capabilities. By following the Demand process, NODs can be submitted for review and approved in a timely fashion (less than a week) which significantly increases likelihood of business success with a level of confidence in IT/Procurement/Security commitment.

Note: As a word of caution, the astute observer will recognize that clever individuals will find ways to circumvent the IT review process and try to reclassify work as either Backlog or POC so as not to have a PM or Architect assigned. This is to be expected because every organization has its non-conformist who wants to exploit demand classifications to satisfy their short-term needs. You want to take the high-road and promote the spirit of collaboration through the IT Review Board because in the long-term, circumventing the process always backfires due to lack of support and ongoing financial commitments (licensing and renewals). By circumventing the IT Review Board weekly funnel, unmanaged work performed in a departmental silo gets lost and only shows-up later when the "mission critical" application breaks and there is no support or funds. At that time, like the arcade game "Whack-a-Mole", you can expose the shadow IT created, whack the deviant miscreant, and remedy the application in a supportable IT model.

After the IT Review Board has approved the work, a PM and an architect are assigned to lead a number of activities (Exhibit 11). The architect will work with the PM on the project kick off deck and determine if a new Architecture is required, and if so, to document in a high-level Solution Design Document (SDD).

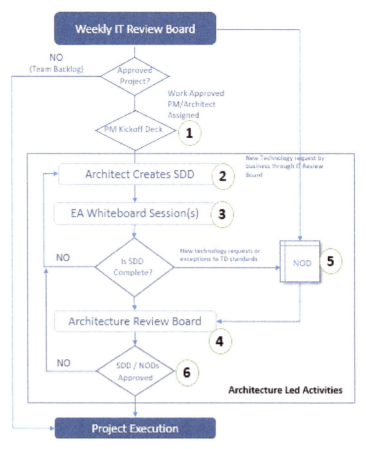

EXHIBIT 11: ENTERPRISE ARCHITECTURE / PMO ALIGNMENT

Project Kickoff Decks are extremely important. Although this is a PMO deliverable to kick off the project, I am always amazed at how many organizations miss this step, or lack consistency in their kickoff decks, by not following a standard project kickoff template.

Projects can be like running a triathlon, long and hot. In a triathlon the first event is the swim, and having a good swim sets the pace for a successful race. The same can be said for the Project Kickoff Deck. The Kickoff Deck sets the pace for the project by getting everyone on the same page. It helps team members get to know each other and shows the project manager's authority and leadership skills. It also helps team members understand the project objectives and allows stakeholders to understand the milestones, risks, assumptions and constraints of the project. Without a proper kickoff, projects run the risk of:

- Inability to complete the project on time and on budget since project team resources are not correctly identified at start and objectives are not clear.
- Lack of established communication channel between client and team.
- Project team inability to respond to changes in business conditions.

On the web site accompanying this book (**www.successful-ea.com**), there is a sample **Project Kickoff Deck** with placeholders for the following:

- Project Goals and Objectives
- High-level business case (approved by Finance)
- RACI identifying team participation levels, roles and responsibilities (Exhibit 12)
- Align on the project timeline and deliverables.

Exhibit 12 is extremely important to the Architect because it defines the core and extended team members that need to participate in the **EA Whiteboard Sessions** explained in the next section.

Roles and Responsibilities

Organization	Participation Level
Business Stakeholders	Approver
Project Management	Approver
Application Delivery	Responsible
Architecture	Consulted/Informed
Infrastructure	Consulted/Informed

Role	Resource(s)
Business Stakeholders	<Who's paying?>
Product Owner	<Who is responsible for success?>
Project Manager	<Who's the PM>
Core Team (Responsible)	Core team members list here
Extended Team (Consulted)	Extended team members list here.

EXHIBIT 12: SAMPLE KICKOFF SLIDE WITH ROLES AND RESPONSIBILITIES

Architecture Review Board (ARB)

The ARB is part of the architecture governance process and acts as a formal gate for architecture approvals to ensure that technical solutions and decisions align to company standards and have considered important contextual factors. An important outcome from the ARB is documenting and approving changes to the Configuration Management Database (CMDB). By implementing an ARB, you are accomplishing an important CMMI criteria for Architecture Governance.

Depending on the size of your organization, setting up an ARB may be scoped at the Line of Business (LOB), regional or global levels. What is important is that the initial executive sponsor of the ARB be at a level to gain high-level corporate support (e.g. CEO, CIO, CTO). As for the recommended size of the ARB, my recommendation is as small as possible with a core set of permanent members. The rationale for a small ARB is, when initially setting it up, there will be a lot of enthusiasm to be "on the ARB board". However, over time, the enthusiasm to attend ARB meetings begins to wane as everyone's normal day job starts to conflict. Techniques like rotating members, or only letting people who attend the ARB vote will fail for various reasons. To keep speed and continuity, and prevent the corporate architecture from varying from one set of ideas to another, the ARB should have one decision maker – either Chief Architect or CIO since they have the most at stake over the long term. ARB meetings must have a routine weekly placeholder on the calendar. To get on the ARB weekly agenda, the assigned architect works with Enterprise Architecture Team.

In summary, the ideal weekly cadence for running an Architect team is the schedule in Table 7. This provides adequate time for the team to anticipate work and communicate results.

TABLE 7: ENTERPRISE ARCHITECT OPERATIONAL CADENCE

Cadence	Meetings	Audience	Purpose	Artifacts
Monday Morning (Weekly)	Internal EA	Enterprise Architects	Review/status upcoming week for Demands, Whiteboards, NODs	Meeting Summary
Tuesday Morning (Weekly)	IT Demand * (Led by IT Demand Coord-inator)	IT Demand Managers EA Leadership	Approve Demands and assign an Architect. (Projects, Assessment, Pilots, POCs, Backlog)	IT Demand provides meeting summary
Tues/Thurs (Weekly)	EA White-board Sessions	Core/Extend ed Project Team	Purpose is to review Architecture Solution Design Documents (SDDs) with core and extended project/architecture team members to validate and align end-to-end solution designs with standards and business needs.	Solution Design Document (SDD) SDD-Lite

Wednesday	Pre-ARB Prep	Enterprise Architects and ARB presenters	Purpose is to pre-review materials for the Thursday ARB meeting. You do not want any surprises since the Thursday meeting should be a rubber stamp.	
Thursday Morning (Weekly)	Archi-tecture Review Board (ARB)	Enterprise Architects Procurement	Request process to formally approve SDDs and/or changes and exceptions to the technology ecosystem and CMDB through a Notice of Decision (NOD).	SDDs Notice of Decision (NOD)

Technology Lifecycles

As vendors update their products, and new security vulnerabilities are identified daily, it is important for Architecture to have a defined lifecycle on each technology element. As a rule of thumb, if the current version of a technology asset is 'N', then you want everything on the IT landscape to be 'N' or 'N-1'. Once an asset becomes 'N-2', you want to work with the PMO to schedule a project to upgrade.

Exhibit 13 defines the typical four phase lifecycle process flow:
- Research
- Adopt
- Mainstream
- Retire

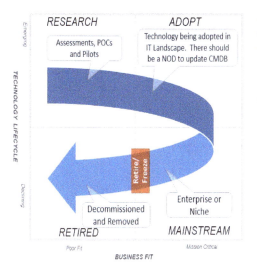

Technology Lifecycle Process
Standardize Process to reduce technical debt and maintain application currency

RESEARCH
Assessments, POCs and Pilots

ADOPT
Technology being adopted in IT Landscape. There should be a NOD to update CMDB

Retire/Freeze

Decommissioned and Removed

RETIRED
Poor Fit

Enterprise or Niche

MAINSTREAM
Mission Critical

BUSINESS FIT

TECHNOLOGY LIFECYCLE

Emerging

Declining

- **Research**: Technology in POC, Pilot or Assessment
- **Adopt**: Technology approved for use in IT Landscape via NOD
- **Mainstream**:
  - Enterprise: Enterprise wide application supported/paid by IT
  - Niche: Business application supported/paid by business
- **Retire**
  - ❑ Target products are to be retired (sunset)
  - ❑ Freeze products are no longer enhanced or invested
  - ❑ Retired products are obsolete

EXHIBIT 13: TECHNOLOGY LIFECYCLE

As covered in the next section, changing the lifecycle status happens in the CMDB and should be done through a NOD so that the decision is documented and communicated to the organization.

****

<u>Take-Away</u>

- ➤ IT Review Board meetings must meet weekly and move fast. All IT work can be categorized in six (6) groups that Architecture is uniquely able to influence.
- ➤ Require Finance to validate all business cases to confirm costs and ROI.
- ➤ All projects must have a PM and an Architect assigned in the IT Review Board to move forward.
- ➤ All projects must have a kick-off deck to clearly define:
  - o Project objectives

53

- o Finance approved business case
- o RACI with defined core and extended team members.
- o Notional project timeline
- ➢ For consistency, speed and prevent the corporate architecture from varying from one set of ideas to another, the ARB should have one decision maker – either Chief Architect or CIO since they have the most at stake over the long term.
- ➢ The ideal weekly Enterprise Architecture operational cadence is:
    - o Monday: Internal Architecture Review for upcoming activities.
    - o Tuesday: Attend IT Review Board to disposition IT Demands Tuesday EA Whiteboard Session
    - o Wednesday: Pre-ARB w/ Chief Architect or CIO to review SDDs and NODs.
    - o Thursday: Attend ARB to approve/reject SDDs and NODs. Thursday EA Whiteboard Session
    - o Friday: Clear your calendar and catch-up.
- ➢ Carefully weigh Architecture involvement in after-the-fact projects that are already behind schedule and over budget. The next chapter recommends an SDD-Lite, but sometimes it is better to throw water on the ashes and start with a fresh business stakeholder and PM.
- ➢ Make sure system decommission plans are part of the overall project scope. Many times, a new solution is implemented as part of a project plan, and the intention is to retire the replaced legacy system in separate project. This rarely happens, and the outcome is you have two systems and technical debt. To avoid this situation, always scope decommissioning in the primary project.

****

Chapter 7 – Domain Architectures: Architecture Deliverables

In this section we will cover architecture deliverables that will make an impact in your career. From the previous chapter, there are six (6) types of work demands that architecture is uniquely able to fulfil. The Architecture goal is to quickly turn these requests around with actionable artifacts so downstream delivery teams can complete on time and under budget. You do not want to be the "long pole in the tent" holding up the rest of the organization. These templates are designed to keep you out of the hot seat and make you successful.

- Solution Design Documents (SDDs)
- Assessments
- Proof of Concept (POC)
- Pilot Charter
- Notice of Decision (NOD)

Solution Design Documents (SDDs)
After the Project Kickoff Deck, the assigned architect will create a TOGAF/ADM inspired **Solution Design Document (SDD)** to capture the business vision, scope, dependencies and risks and then document the current and goal state architectures for each of the TOGAF Architecture domains (Business, Data, Application, Technology) as shown in Exhibit 14.

TOGAF Inspired Solution Design Document

- • Phase A – Architecture Vision

- • Business Needs

- • Stakeholder Concerns

- • Key Drivers / Principles

Phases B-D

- • Business Architecture (Phase B)

- • Data Architecture (Phase C)

- • Application Architecture (Phase C)

- • Infrastructure Architecture (Phase D)

- • Security Architecture

Phase F - Migration Planning

Phase G – Implementation Governance

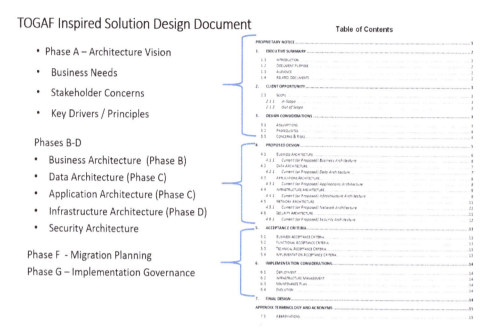

EXHIBIT 14: TOGAF INSPIRED SOLUTION DESIGN DOCUMENT (SDD) TABLE OF CONTENTS

The contents of this document will read like a newspaper article. Starting with a high-level Executive Summary, subsequent sections provide lower-level details appealing to technical audiences.

- • Executive Summary, Client Opportunities and Design Considerations are written to appeal to business stakeholders and executive leadership so there is a clear understanding of the business benefit, project value and scope.

- • Proposed Design section should be more granular and consider each of the TOGAF ADM domains and written to the level of detail that assigned Subject Matter Experts (SMEs) in the project delivery phase can understand and appreciate.

- • Acceptance Criteria and Maintenance Considerations are the final sections and should clearly define project success expectations for each domain as well as maintenance and support considerations. Many projects get to the finish line only to discover the expected support team was not aware of the resources and budget to maintain. I recall one project that was set for a Friday night deployment. Everyone was excited and executives were on-hand for success; except no one told the firewall engineers. Someone could have written a thesis on group depression that night when no data made it through the firewalls. It is important to get such items documented in the SDD to avoid gaps in communications and planning as solutions go-live.

The SDD should also be technical with no sales fluff. Many times, there is a tendency by the SDD author to copy-n-paste wording from a vendor website to compensate content detail. This is a mistake. It is important that the SDD author understand design details and considerations at low levels to lead meetings and discussions with knowledge experts.

As shown in Exhibit 15, the SDD format is flexible and not a one size fits all proposition. In the perfect world, the full SDD document is recommended because it allows for maximum time to flush-out the design and goal state architecture. However, you never want Architecture to block business progress; therefore, you can streamline the SDD documentation process a couple ways.

Solution Design Document Formats

Full SDD

- Follows TOGAF ADM to document current state/goal state architecture domains that are part of the solution.
- Identifies business vision, drivers, risk and assumptions.
- Provides input to downstream implementation teams: Infrastructure needs, firewall rules, service accounts, integrations, runbooks, etc..

SDD (Lite)

- After-the-fact SDDs where we need to document a solution quickly that has been implemented outside IT Review Board but requires IT involvement.
- Architecture section to provide what is the real recommended approach.

Wiki SDD Format

- Same format as Full SDD but in a wiki site.
- Good for long running, cross-business efforts with multiple workstreams and stakeholders.

EXHIBIT 15: SDD FORMATS

- **SDD (Lite)**: Sometimes the business starts activities without Architecture involvement. Architecture is brought in after-the-fact to validate a business purchased technology and/or at the request of the project manager (PM) since the project is already behind schedule and over budget. In these circumstances, an SDD (Lite) is a great alternative to quickly get the entire project team onboard and engaged in an end-to-end goal state architecture. SDD (Lite) still adheres to the TOGAF ADM format, but is slimmed down to only capture the necessary details. At the top of the SDD (Lite) is a section for the Architecture Recommendation. This allows the Architecture team to weigh-in on what the recommended solution/approach should have been in case there is a misalignment with standards.

- **Wiki SDD** is another channel to document solution designs. Wiki format is best for long running projects that are cross-departmental and can spin-off many sub-project efforts that could themselves benefit from a solution design. With the wiki format, sub-projects can be linked together to show cross-functional dependencies.

Whichever SDD format you choose, the draft SDD should go through a mandatory two (2) EA Whiteboard review sessions with core and extended project team members identified from the Project Kickoff Deck. EA Whiteboard Sessions are intended to be collaborative; allowing the team to step through each section of the SDD and confirm alignment with proposed business and technical requirements, impacts to other domains, and adherence to target state architecture and architectural principles. EA Whiteboard Sessions do not need to be confined to just project team members. You should also include other SMEs and influencers who are not afraid to ask questions or poke holes in the solution. The more eyes on the SDD, the better the results and final product. Additional EA Whiteboard Sessions may be required as the solution design evolves and/or as cross-domain impacts are negotiated in response to input up through a final review in the Architecture Review Board (ARB).

A final story on the importance of a full SDD. At one point in my career, I joined a startup company to develop a content and delivery system for retail clients. Initially there were only three of us doing the design and development work across the different tiers: front-end user interface, middle-tier processing and backend data and analytics. We worked well as a team and spent many long nights and weekends designing and developing the initial product. Unfortunately, we did not take many notes documenting our key design choices since many of the important decisions were made very late at night over old coffee and cold pizza. Regardless, we were successful and the initial release was a huge success and the company grew.

As more people joined the company, there were requests for new functionality and questions from new developers on why certain design decisions were made. Without a documented solution design capturing details and decision points, some of our important midnight choices were lost with the coffee cups and pizza boxes they were drawn. On one particular topic, we forgot why we did something a certain way and decided to modify the design. Unfortunately, six months later we hit a technical roadblock that made us revert back to the original design. The epiphany moment for me was we discovered this roadblock months earlier during a midnight pizza box design session, but forgot and never wrote it down. We lost almost one year of work because we did not take the time to create and maintain a full solution design.

The moral of the story is that a detailed solution design document might be laborious to create and maintain, but it will pay huge dividends later when team amnesia strikes and/or new team members join and ask questions.

Assessments

In the spirit of keeping the IT Review Board meeting moving fast and efficient, assessments are useful when there needs to be a better understanding and/or guidance on a topic before a formal work decision can be made. By Architecture raising their hand and offering to lead these assessments promotes the technology thought leader role. Assessments can be categorized as either "Quick" or "Detailed" Assessments (Exhibit 16).

Assessment Types

Quick Assessment Deliverable   Full Assessment Deliverable

EXHIBIT 16: ASSESSMENT FORMATS

To keep things simple, assessments are scored on a 1-5 scale with 1 being the horrible and 5 being the great. A zero (0) is used to abstain.

1. **Show Stopper** - The solution is completely infeasible or outside the budget and breaks company standards and/or best practices.
2. **Poor Fit** - This solution does not meet company standards and technical guidelines but could work with enough resources.
3. **Average Fit** – Most common rating for viable solution options.
4. **Good Fit** – This solution aligns with company standards and technical guidelines.
5. **Perfect Fit** – This rating is usually reserved for options that already exist within the company, and are currently supported and covered in budget. There is little to no financial or personal overhead to implement this option.

If scoring on a 1 to 5 scale is too controversial, one can substitute Harvey balls for numbers. Harvey balls are round ideograms used to visually communicate qualitative information. An empty Harvey ball represents 1 and a solid equals 5.

| 1 = Show Stopper | 2 = Poor Fit | 3 = Average Fit | 4 = Good Fit | 5 = Perfect Fit |

a) **Quick Assessments** generally take less than eight (8) hours to complete and are used when Architecture needs to quickly weigh-in on a given approach. The deliverable is typically a slide deck. The critical slide is the **Evaluation Matrix** qualifying the recommendation over five (5) criteria: Cost over three (3) years, Architecture Fit, Business Fit, Quality, Security/Risk. To evaluate in less than eight (8) hours, there are some important assumptions to make:

- Scoring is done on a scale of 1 to 5 with 1 being horrible and 5 being a perfect fit.
- All five (5) criteria are considered equal and receive the same 20% weighting.
- The architect works alone to compile an unbiased assessment appraisal.

The final deliverable is a slide deck with three (3) to five (5) slides containing:
- Assessment overview and objectives at the executive level.
- Business Context Diagram showing the overall scope including: investment, impacted business processes, key stakeholders and any interfaces.
- Solution options analysis with pros/cons supporting the Evaluation Matrix (Exhibit 17)
- Evaluation Matrix scoring the solution over the five (5) categories.
- Summary slide with Architecture Recommendations and Next Steps.

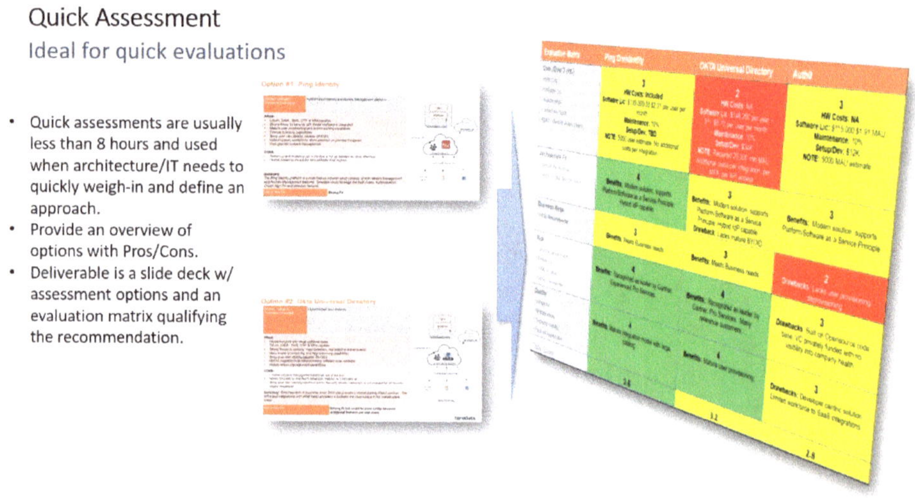

Quick Assessment
Ideal for quick evaluations

- Quick assessments are usually less than 8 hours and used when architecture/IT needs to quickly weigh-in and define an approach.
- Provide an overview of options with Pros/Cons.
- Deliverable is a slide deck w/ assessment options and an evaluation matrix qualifying the recommendation.

EXHIBIT 17: QUICK ASSESSMENT OPTION ANALYSIS

b) **Detailed Assessments** involve coordination of multiple vendor demos and weighted scoring by stakeholders. For this reason, Detailed Assessments generally take six (6) weeks to complete and are run as a project with an assigned PM, Kickoff Deck and core team members who provide assessment requirements and solution/vendor scoring. Architects should never try and "PM" a detailed assessment due to the coordination required to schedule demos and gather requirements from all the stakeholders. These are tasks better managed by the PMO. Instead, the architect should use the templates shown in Exhibit 18 and found on the web site to speed the assessment process.

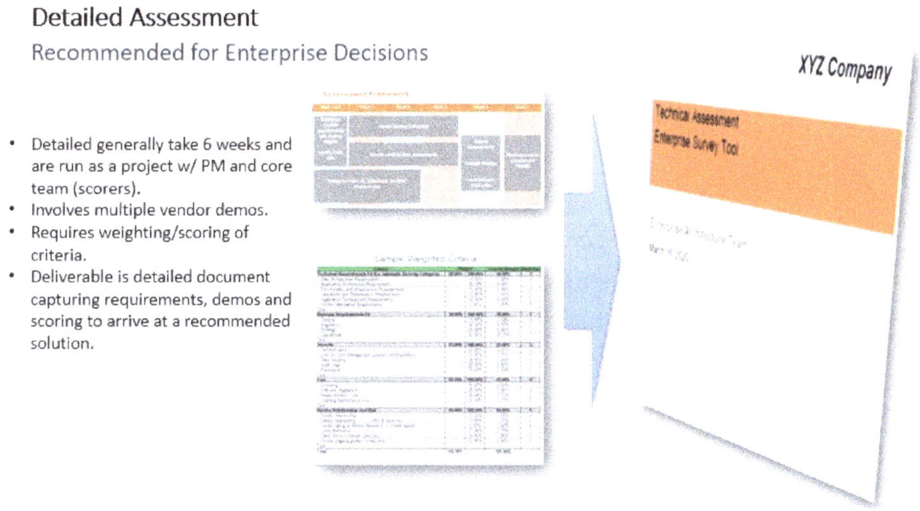

EXHIBIT 18: DETAILED ASSESSMENT

- **Assessment Framework** is a kickoff deck to get all the team members on the same page for objectives, roles, responsibilities and timeframes.
- **Weighted Spreadsheet:** Working with the PM and other core team members, the Architect will gather requirements for each of the five (5) criteria: Cost over three (3) years, Architecture Fit, Business Fit, Quality, Security/Risk and put in a

spreadsheet. The spreadsheet allows the ability to assign weights to requirements so some requirements can carry more weight than others. For example, if "Business Fit" is more critical than "Cost", then "Business Fit" can be weighted 30% value while "Cost" is adjusted to 10%. Once weighting is complete, the spreadsheet is distributed back to team members and vendors to facilitate demo agenda and scoring. (Of course, be sensitive to what vendors can see).

- **Detailed Technical Assessment Document:** At the conclusion of all demos, the Architect gathers all the spreadsheet scorecards and compiles the findings in the Detailed Technical Assessment document. This document usually finds its way to an executive, so spend quality time writing and analyzing findings. A well written Detailed Technical Assessment document will pay dividends for the EA Team since they can serve as a reference point for many years. I had one Detailed Technical Assessment document whose findings were referenced by both IT and the Business for over five (5) years as company employees churned and priorities changed, but the fundamental business requirements stayed the same thus validating the assessment recommendations.

Pilot: Similar to a POC; however, a successful Pilot can proceed to production. To qualify for success, a Pilot must have a **Pilot Charter** document (Exhibit 19) that identifies the pilot's objectives and between 5-10 success criteria to measure outcomes. Pilots are useful for teams to try a solution and then go-live. Pilots should be time bound less than 90 days with the team reporting back the Pilot Charter results for final decision. A PM and Architect should be assigned to make sure the Pilot follows the process.

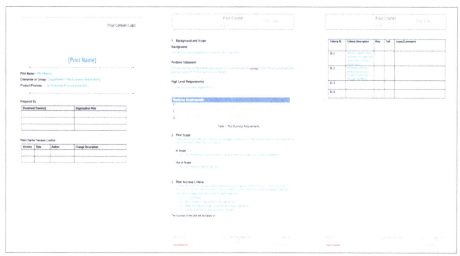

EXHIBIT 19: PILOT CHARTER TEMPLATE

Notice of Decision (NOD): A NOD (Exhibit 20) is designed to fill the gap in the Demand process by allowing the business a formal method for requesting changes and/or exceptions to IT standards and/or the Configuration Management Database (CMDB) which stores information about approved hardware and software assets. A NOD is a notification, not a solution, and secures a high-level understanding of business need, approach, funding and level of impact to IT, Procurement and Security. NODs help reduce technical debt by providing transparency and justification for business requests that may overlap with existing capabilities. By following the Demand process, NODs can be submitted for review and approved in a timely fashion (less than a week) which significantly increases likelihood of business success with a level of confidence in IT/Procurement/Security commitment.

Notice of Decision   [Your Company Logo]

The purpose of this document is to allow for architectural review of new solution designs and design elements that deviate from accepted company IT standards.

Decision ID:	[Filled in when approved.]
Date:	<Enter date>
Title:	<Enter Title>
Type of NOD:	Request one of the following: ☐Solution Design ☐Pilot ☐Notification
Framework:	Request one of the following as a primary framework: ☐Application ☐ Data Center ☐ Desktop ☐Network ☐Security
End of Life or End of Support Date:	<Enter applicable date>
Approval for exception expires on and must be reviewed:	<Enter date that the NOD would expire and need to be reviewed again. Typically, 3-6 months>
Estimated document delivery date:	<Enter the date that a solution design or other document will be available for review>
Affected applications or environments:	<Enter name of impacted application/service>
Problem Statement:	Background: <Provide an executive summary of the issue and why a NOD is needed>

Recommended Solution:	<Provide an executive summary of the recommended solution and why it is required. The following are helpful questions to be answered>
	1. What is the expected Start/End Date?
	2. Describe Scope of Work/Responsibilities
	3. Describe following...
	    a. Who is doing Installation?
	    b. Who is the use audience /Number of users?
	    c. How are users authenticating/accessing the tool?
	    d. Is this a SaaS solution or do we need to install software?
	    e. What is the data classification the tool is capturing?
	    f. Is the data going outside the organization?
	    g. Is there a financial business case? What's the ROI?
	4. Describe ongoing expected cost and who is paying?
	5. Describe Support Model?

Contacts:	<Enter the business and vendor contacts >
Documents included as part of the NOD:	<List documents that accompanied the NOD like a solution design or a Pilot Charter>
Summary and basis for decision:	<Write an executive level decision for either approving or rejecting the NOD. The decision should come from ARB to provide coverage. >

EXHIBIT 20: NOTICE OF DECISION (NOD) TEMPLATE

****

Take-Away

➢ Although, detailed assessments are more democratic, I have found quick assessments to be as effective for selecting the best solution.
➢ Anytime there is an IT exception request or change to the CMDB, document in a NOD and post in the Architecture Repository (Chapter 9). Capturing the business need, approach, funding level and impact to IT, Procurement and Security will pay huge dividends when amnesia strikes at annual planning meetings: "I thought IT was buying and supporting this in the future?"

➢ As mentioned in the previous chapter, carefully weigh Architecture involvement in after-the-fact projects that are already behind schedule and over budget. These are usually no-win situations, but if you must get involved, write an SDD-Lite and document the Architecture Recommendation.

****

Chapter 8 – Vision: Landscapes, Viewpoints and Patterns

Being a successful leader means there will always be challenges, and in a rapidly changing digital world, there are a number of top issues on executive minds which require coordinated, cross-functional tangible solutions.   Be it endless variations of the same problems or new obstacles to keep you on your guard like:

- The growing demand for a mobile and remote workforce.
- Customer churn. Inaccurate reports and forecast.
- Record-breaking cybersecurity and ransomware attacks; and
- Moving to the cloud.

Given the urgency and intensity of today's business problems, executive leaders are eager to embrace solutions in rapid timelines that can be quickly implemented and scaled up. Unfortunately, there's a tremendous gap between executive expectations and the reality that IT, the business and other changemakers can deliver. The resources, ecosystems, and growth prospects at most companies are vastly different than those available to companies like Microsoft, Tesla and Google.

To solve today's most complex and urgent problems, **IT Landscape Models, Architecture Viewpoints** and **Reference Patterns** are important tools for you to document viable approaches.   These artifacts become important elements of the **Enterprise Architecture Reference Repository** to act as a directional guide for others.   By providing a landscape overview, vision and approved recommended approach to solve some of the businesses most difficult technical challenges, architects gain leverage in being thought leaders, influence architecture road maps and company strategy/direction.

- **IT Landscape Models** (aka, The Fridge) provides a straightforward method to conceptually capture the IT Landscape (or any other focus area) broken down into four (4) main components: Security, User

68

perspective, Technology stack and Operations/Support. By scoping the landscape in a box (or Fridge) pattern, you can quickly identify solution gaps and ask important questions necessary to bolster the solution.

- **Architecture Viewpoints** (aka, Position Papers, Point-of-Views, Decision Points, 1-Pager) offer a documented heading specifically addressing a particular point of view in the organization. Many technology decisions are poorly documented or happen by unintended/unconscious evolution. Relations between business needs, decisions, and architectural elements are missing, and architecture alternatives are not preserved. Viewpoints present concise documented architecture recommendations, together with related analysis of current/future requirements and architectural elements to arrive at a desired target state architecture and design decision.

- **Reference Patterns** are pre-approved logical models of technical solutions for the IT Landscape. Similar to Viewpoints, many times technology decisions are poorly documented or happen by evolution. As a consequence, it is hard to identify solutions that should have been deprecated when requirements change. Patterns fill this gap and can be thought of as blueprints that identify components at the logical and design level with security provisions for data flow, interactivity and relationships. Design Patterns are intended to be enduring, speed the design process and to be reused across the company.

IT Landscape Model:
Aka "The Fridge" is one of my favorite models because it provides an uncomplicated outline of the end-to-end solution landscape covering four (4) main critical areas: Security, User perspective, Operations & Support and the Technical stack. As shown Exhibit 21, the Fridge helps you get your head around the entire solution scope and ask specific questions about those four views. To understand the Fridge, study it as a box with Security on the left,

Users on top, Operation & Maintenance on the right and the Technical stack going from bottom to top.

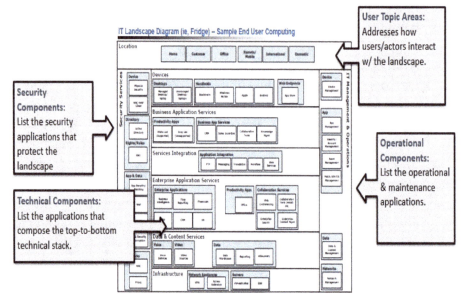

EXHIBIT 21: SAMPLE IT LANDSCAPE (AKA FRIDGE) MODEL

- **User Reference** takes the user perspective into account based on user types, their locations and the number of users. Understanding the who, what, how and how many has important implications on security and licensing. For each user type, you want to capture the following information:
  - How many users? (important for licensing)
  - What location(s) and where are users accessing?
  - What types of users (employees, customers, suppliers, etc.)?
  - What devices are users using (mobile, web, computers, etc.)?

- **Security Reference** identifies the security technologies that protect the landscape. Components you want to identify are how user identities are stored, security and components to safeguard user/data access (i.e.

VPNs, Firewalls, Gateways, Reverse Proxies). Questions you want to answer are:

- How are user identities being stored, authenticated, authorized?
- What security devices and control points are protecting the solution?

- **Operations & Maintenance (O&M)** includes the applications used for day-to-day monitoring and management of the users, systems and equipment. Frequently O&M is overlooked, or assumed to fall under another department. Successful O&M requires participation and cooperation on multiple levels and cannot succeed without everyone involved understanding the basic support structure. Questions you want to answer are:

- What applications are used to monitor and manage the solution end-to-end?
- What support groups are involved and their service levels?

- **Technology Reference** is the layered top-to-bottom combination of business applications, tools, integration interfaces and infrastructure used to support the client-side (front-end) and server-side (back-end) solution. Your technology stack should be aligned with your Architecture Principles in Chapter 5. For example, if you have a Principle such as, "Control Technical Diversity", your technical stack model should represent an IT ecosystem that maximizes reuse and preferred partner solutions. Any overlapping functionality from multiple vendors without a justifiable business competitive advantage is considered technical debt and should be retired from the landscape.

In addition to a clean holistic landscape view, the flexibility of the Fridge model is something you will find appealing because it can be used in a number of circumstances. It is a great compliment to Chapter 7 to reinforce your solution design document by providing an overview of the current state architecture and the future state architecture. Often you might see a Fridge-type diagram with company logos to help identify key functional investments, lines to show data flows and/or a legend to denote technologies lifecycles. (Legends are referenced in Chapter 11).

Architecture Viewpoints:

A Viewpoint presents Architecture's documented position on an issue. The goal is to convince the audience that your EA analysis is accurate with actionable next steps. The intended audience for Viewpoints is the C-level; therefore, positions need to be carefully considered, the argument developed, and the paper organized to support findings. It is very important to address all sides of the issue and present it in a manner that is easy for the audience to understand. Your recommendations and analysis must show you have well-founded knowledge of the topic being presented. You want to persuade the audience to execute the next steps.

Because executive leadership wants to embrace solutions quickly without reading pages of analysis, Viewpoints must fit on one-page (i.e. 1-Pager) and never more than two pages. As a consultant, I would charge $5-$10K for a typical whitepaper, but up to ten times that amount for a concise Viewpoint. Exhibit 22 shows a sample Viewpoint format that I have found resonates best with executives.

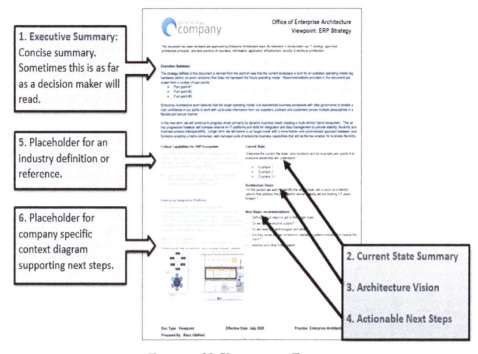

EXHIBIT 22: VIEWPOINT FORMAT

- **Executive Summary** has a dual purpose: to introduce the topic piquing the reader's interest and also recommending the preferred architecture approach. An effective method to accomplish this is by listing known organizational pain-points in context with cost, productivity, efficiency impacts. It is important to support your argument with evidence to ensure the validity of your claims, as well as to refute any counterclaims. The goal is to show that you are well informed about both sides. A good closing line to the Executive Summary is:

  "The Enterprise Architecture team believes that having a well-managed [insert recommendation] is an important enabler for [insert problem being solved] and supports [insert Architecture Principle(s)] throughout the enterprise."

- **Current State** elaborates on the pain-points in the Executive Summary and is supported by a future state gap analysis. The section should address what would happen if the status quo is maintained. Do not be afraid to reference the CMMI maturity models to support the view that the current state is not optimum.

- **Architecture Vision**. In the Architecture Vision, the reader must have a sense that the architecture argument is stronger than the current state or any opposing arguments. For counterarguments, consider one or two points of what someone might say who disagrees with you. Can you reject the counterargument and explain why it is mistaken? Either way, be charitable summarizing opposing opinions. Present each argument fairly and objectively, rather than attack. This is an executive-level paper; therefore, you want to show that you have fairly and seriously considered all sides of the issue, and that you are not simply mocking a bad decision.

- **Next Steps**. Provide an actionable set of next steps that others can rally around. Restate the topic and conclusions and do not introduce new information.

- **Industry Reference** provides an area to insert an accepted industry reference or topic definition from a reputable source. This will help establish you have researched the topic with proven sources like Gartner or McKinsey and provided their definition, not your own. You want this in the top-left below the Executive Summary since the readers natural reading progression will be top-down, left-to-right.

- **Business Context** provides organization context by relating the viewpoint directly to your organization. A contextual high-level business diagram from your SDD is excellent to help connect the dots between your recommendation and your organization.

Reference Patterns:

When documenting patterns, you are not interested in detailing specific physical devices or software; rather you are more interested in establishing the connection between business process and architecture decisions with designs that illustrate how technology components need to be placed and interact to deliver approved functionality. Patterns are an important tool for architects since they illustrate conceptual/logical architectural approaches that can be applied to the organization as a whole and reused across multiple departments. Additionally, they provide specific guidance for solution designers and implementers on how technologies need to interoperate. Without reference patterns, delivery teams can become pioneers and start blazing new technology trails causing IT silos, technical debt and security vulnerabilities.

Exhibit 23 shows a typical web pattern for external access to public data and external access to sensitive date. In these patterns you are interested in showing the recommended web server infrastructure, security zone layout, network architecture (ports/protocols) and how the components interoperate and work together based on the classification of the data (public data or sensitive data). For patterns to be relevant over time, they typically show technology capabilities required but usually not products (unless the product is a standard).

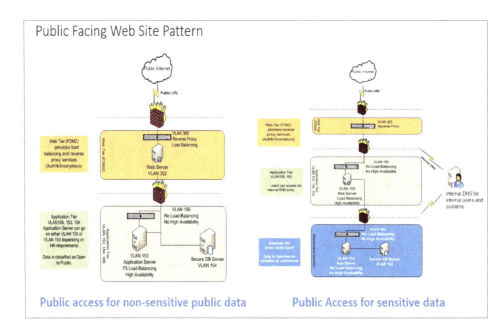

EXHIBIT 23: SAMPLE WEB PATTERN

Each pattern is accompanied by a description that identifies the key components of the pattern and the interaction of the components as well as providing any relevant background information that may be useful in understanding the pattern and how it applies within the business. Patterns do not represent detailed designs for solutions which must be determined based on specific business requirements, but they do represent a vetted and pre-approved understanding from Architecture and IT (Networking, Security, Infrastructure) that reusing the pattern in a solution speeds the design process. When writing a Solution Design Document (SDD) and performing an EA Whiteboard, using an approved pattern simplifies the discussion because there is no need to debate the solution. As long as the solution is shown to adhere to an approved Architecture Pattern, then you can continue to the next topic.

In summary, Architecture Patterns are important in that they:

76

- Communicates enterprise-wide technology approaches
  - Documents the consensus established by participants on technology standards.
  - Provides all stakeholders and supporting delivery teams with guidance on the strategic direction for technology usage.
- Accelerates and standardizes the technology design
  - Provides technologists with logical patterns for the design and implementation of technology infrastructure.
  - Provides application owners and developers with guidance on technology choices.
- Fosters ongoing collaboration
  - Establishes a common language for defining and describing technology standards and usage.
  - Provides artifacts that can be used for technology planning.
  - Serves as a template for planning and documenting standards.

****

Take-Away

- ➢ Viewpoints are challenging to write. Plan on spending six weeks to accurately and concisely get your thoughts on paper.
- ➢ Architecture Patterns provide an approved standardized approach that speeds design and delivery by maximizing reuse.
- ➢ Landscape models, Viewpoints and Architecture Patterns are important artifacts in the Architecture Repository because they organize knowledge and connect important business features required for planning and management. These will be popular artifacts in your repository.

****

Chapter 9 - EA Change Management: Reference Repository

Although we are striving to be data driven, operating a mature Architecture capability within a large company creates a significant volume of architectural output. Effective document management of these architectural work products requires a system that facilitates ease of storage, access, collaboration and the ability for others to discover and find relevant architecture content. Discovery is important, because like all organizations, collective amnesia can strike months or even years after an important decision has been made. There is scientific evidence backing memory (or lack of memory) playing a key role in poor decision-making. Due to the volume of IT activities and meetings taking place, many decision-making processes are unconscious and automatic. Individuals choose among alternatives and memory is susceptible to bias. Information about what was recalled in the past is often used for future decisions. This section describes the structural outline for an **Enterprise Architecture Reference Repository** that allows storage of different architectural assets and acts as a source of truth on important IT decisions.

The EA Repository is central to the Architecture organization, providing a formal taxonomy to differentiate different architectural assets. The EA Repository needs to have two views: the external public-facing view for approved deliverables created in Chapter 5-8 and the internal-facing site for internal team collaboration and reference materials (Exhibit 24).

- **Public-facing** for published collective works, shared reference artifacts and documentation with IT and business partners that provide transparency and competitive advantage to the business.
- **Internal-facing** drafts and architecture team collaboration. This site should only be for individual contributors to architecture content.

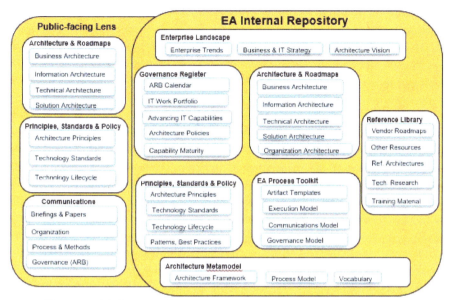

EXHIBIT 24: SAMPLE REFERENCE ARCHITECTURE REPOSITORY

At a high level, the following types of architectural information are expected to be held and discoverable within an Architecture Repository:

- **Architecture Landscape and Roadmaps** contain a complete architectural representation of current/future state architecture models for the organization and transformational roadmaps. A good visual is your organizations APQC Capability Map. Preferably this is also a drill-down (since you are data driven) for easy access linking recognized department capabilities, processes, applications and data objects.
- **Principles, Standards and Policies** contain Architecture Principles, Reference Architectures, View Points, EA engagement models and processes that support governance of the Enterprise Architecture.
- **Solution Designs and Assessments** contain approved SDDs and Assessments.
- **NODs, Pilots and POC's** capture decisions around how new products and services were evaluated.

- **EA Reference Library** contain templates, guidelines, patterns, and other forms of reference material that can be leveraged in order to accelerate the creation of new architectures for the organization.

Tactically, the public facing view of the Architecture Reference Repository should be hosted on your company's primary Intranet, communications and collaboration platform. The rationale is you want to reach the largest population with access to EA materials through search and self-service. If you can get an internal DNS entry to point to your site – even better (e.g. https://ea.companydomain.com)

****
Take-Away

- ➢ The Architecture Reference Repository should be hosted on your company's primary Intranet, communications and collaboration platform for easy, searchable access by the rest of the company.
- ➢ Secure a memorable DNS name for your EA site so there is a simple connection to your URL and content.
  - ○ Ex) https://ea.companydomain.com

****

PART THREE – The Living Enterprise Architecture

Welcome to Part 3. In this section you will be using the architecture frameworks, principles and deliverables to create the Living Architecture View. This is an active 360 degree view of your organization's processes, applications and IT landscape. With this field of vision, you can quickly answer executive leadership questions that would normally take weeks to understand and require a small archeology dig to uncover.

Cost Management:
- Are we investing according to strategy?
- What capabilities are over budget?
- What is the cost of IT? Marketing? Sales? How do these compare to industry peers?

Security/Standards:
- Are we aligned with standards and using approved software?
- Are we architecturally compliant and secure?
- What is our software/hardware/business lifecycle and roadmap?

Impact/Dependencies:
- What is the impact of change to the business?
- Can we do 'what if' scenarios for planning?

Transformation:
- What business capabilities are strategic versus those that can be retired or commoditized?
- What applications can be rationalized?
- What applications/services can be transformed?

As a reminder from Chapter 3, to be Level 4 CMMI compliant, the Living Architecture View requires an architecture tool for capturing and mapping IT assets and systems across the business. Examples in Chapters 10-12 assume you have some automation in place to properly mine and dashboard IT metrics.

Chapter 10 - Applications to Capability Mapping

From Chapter 2, the first step in creating the Living Enterprise Architecture is to inventory and catalog the Business Capabilities that define your company. You will utilize the APQC spreadsheet that you downloaded for your industry segment. With an impetus for speed, you start with the first three (3) APQC levels which are the **Level 1 Category**, **Level 2 Process Group** and **Level 3 Process**. In the downloaded APQC spreadsheet, you should have also added a column to assign a business owner for each element. Using your architecture tool, upload the spreadsheet to start creating the Capability Map (Exhibit 25). The Capability Map provides a complete panoramic view of all your organizations capabilities and sub-capabilities that achieve your corporate goals. By stocktaking and assessing your business capabilities, you get an understanding of what capabilities provide competitive differentiation, as well as which are missing or at risk. This is the basis for Capability-based planning (CBP) and helps focus IT on the continuous creation of business value. Organizations with superior capabilities to execute their strategy will win.

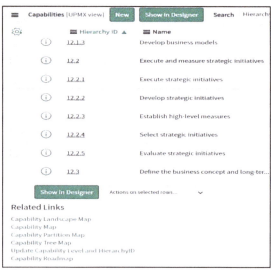

EXHIBIT 25: UPLOADED APQC SPREADSHEET TO SERVICENOW® SOFTWARE

ServiceNow is a registered trademark of ServiceNow Inc.

Once uploaded, perform these steps:

A) Step through each capability and create relationships between the capabilities, business processes and supporting applications.

B) Setup meetings with each business owner. It is important to have a communication plan with each owner to solicit their input and support. Start with an initial meeting and then, at a minimum, quarterly sync-ups to get their feedback. Within three (3) months working with business owners, you should have a complete draft of business capabilities and their lifecycles (Exhibit 26).

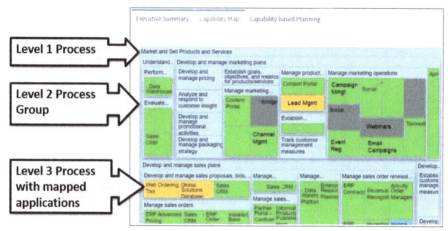

EXHIBIT 26: CAPABILITY MAP IN SERVICENOW/INS-PI DESIGNER®

Key points from Exhibit 26 are:

(1) APQC Level 1 Categories (i.e. Capabilities) are listed on top.
(2) APQC Level 2 Process Groups are listed under their corresponding capabilities.
(3) APQC Level 3 Processes are listed below the hierarchy. Applications and their status are combined with their main business processes.

Ins-pi Designer is a trademark of ins-pi GmbH.

83

With some creativity, you can tune business capability views by department, strategic importance and/or lifecycle to engage any audience (Exhibit 27).

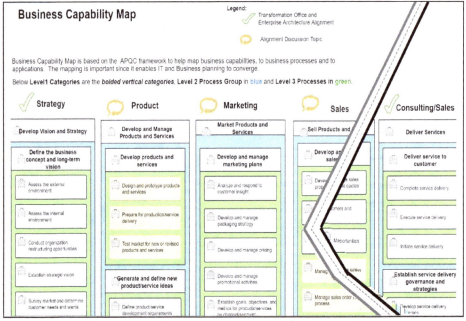

EXHIBIT 27: CAPABILITY MAP BY DEPARTMENT

****

Take-Away

➢ Business Capability Mapping accelerates the business and IT planning cycle by providing visibility into what capabilities provide competitive differentiation, can be considered commodities, or missing and at risk.

➢ A capability-centric organization overcomes the common problem of organizational silos, shadow IT and technical debt by identifying and eliminating corporate-wide redundancies.

****

Chapter 11 - Applications to Business Process Mapping

After successfully uploading Business Capabilities in Chapter 10, your next step is to model the Application Portfolio by mapping applications to capabilities and business processes. This step helps you track business applications that directly support business processes and the organization investment strategy. As an architect, you need to be conversant in explaining business processes and applications as they tie to the business strategy and opportunities for improvement. Application Portfolio Management (APM) allows you to:

- Sort, group and view applications by category, lifecycle, cost, location to understand application costs and end-of-support/retirement dates.
- Analyze the application categories and assess relevance and alignment to business strategy.
- Identify opportunities to reduce costs, fill gaps in meeting organization goals, and submit IT Demands to kick-off remediation projects.

Since a picture is worth a thousand words, Exhibit 28 is a good business process example that can be used in EA Whiteboard sessions and deliverables. This format has been proven to resonate with executive business stakeholders and tactical implementation teams to understand the end-to-end processes to get a holistic view of scope and impact. In an actual online whiteboard session, boxes 3 to 5 are dynamically generated from the CMDB (hence the Living Architecture) and are clickable to support lower level granular drilldowns.

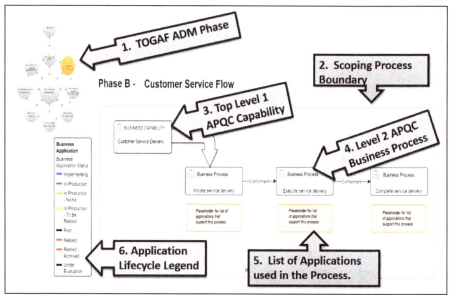

EXHIBIT 28: SAMPLE TOGAF CAPABILITY WITH SUPPORTING BUSINESS PROCESSES

Key points from Exhibit 28 are:

(1) The TOGAF ADM phase is denoted in the model to reconfirm the value that the TOGAF methodology brings to the architecture process. In the above example, we clearly identify this as a Phase B Business Architecture deliverable.

(2) Unless you want your EA whiteboard sessions to go down the proverbial rathole, always provide a scoping boundary for models (in red dashed-line). The boundary defines the measurable and auditable characteristics of what is being discussed and determines the limits and exclusions of what is expected.

(3) APQC Level 2 Process Group defined as your Business Capability. The capability and business process flow names come from the APQC spreadsheet.

(4) APQC Level 3 Business Processes that support (3)

(5) List of Business Applications that support the Level 3 Business Processes. This list should be generated directly from the CMDB and reconfirmed with the identified business process owner you noted in your APQC spreadsheet.

(6) All business applications go through a technology lifecycle: Research, Adopt, Mainstream, Retire. The NOD process is used to define technology lifecycle changes so there is global awareness.

To highlight the drilldown concept, if you were to click in the business process box #4 in Exhibit 28 for "Initiate Service Delivery", your audience will expect to see a representation of the lower-level sub-process similar to Exhibit 29. In this example, you have gone a level deeper by mapping the business sub-processes with the applications, logical interfaces and data that are required to support the process. Visually it looks very similar to Exhibit 28, but with more granularity. You can continue this drill-down process to support all the TOGAF ADM artifacts appropriate for the solution.

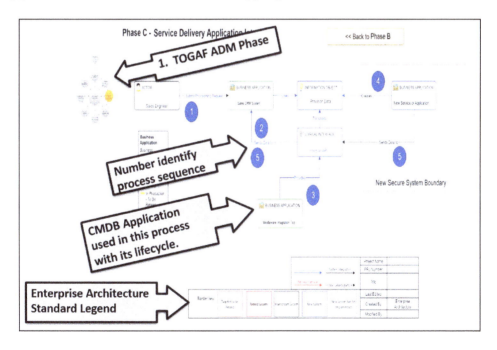

Key points from Exhibit 29 are:

(1) The TOGAF ADM phase is denoted in the title.
(2) Process steps are numbered so your audience understands the process flow.
(3) Business Applications that support the Business Processes are generated directly from the CMDB and color-coded based on their lifecycle.
(4) Standard Enterprise Architecture legend and color key (Exhibit 30) to help designate additional information like location, if in project scope, integrations, etc. I like the following color codes:
   a. **Black** = Existing system or capability and no change
   b. Solid Blue = New system or capability and in-scope
   c. Dash Blue = New system or capability and out-of-scope
   d. Red = System to be retired.

EXHIBIT 30: ARCHITECTURE LEGEND AND COLOR KEY

Obviously, there are some personal tastes for the colors, but the important point is to have a standard color set on each model. It is confusing when the Architecture team uses red for retirement and some other group is using purple and orange.

Mapping Applications to Business Processes

Relationship mapping is a never-ending activity and requires someone to own and manage. However, it provides tremendous benefits to the organization and makes the Living Architecture a reality. The EA team should govern and monitor relationship management upkeep. To be clear, application data integrity is still the responsibility of identified Application owner who should be updating their data each quarter to maintain application lifecycles, support models, maintenance contacts and renewal dates/costs. With a well-managed application portfolio, additional automations can be triggered to send out ticklers/service requests to application owners when updates are due. You can also digitally badge application data considered current to signify data quality. By performing systematic management of the technology portfolio, you can optimize expenses, identify redundancies in applications, and also retire application technologies that are expensive to maintain.

****

<u>Take-Away</u>

➢ With support from the CFO/COO/CIO:
- o Enterprise Architecture must govern and monitor Application Portfolio Management (APM).
- o Application owners must be held responsible for updating their CMDB application data on routine intervals.

➢ A well-managed application portfolio enables opportunities to reduce costs, fill process and capability gaps, and submit IT Demands to kick-off projects.

➢ As mentioned in Chapter 2, having a well-managed application portfolio accelerates merger and acquisition (M&A) activities by providing an accurate inventory of business technologies necessary for IT to support post M&A integrations and data sharing.

****

Chapter 12 – Living Architecture View: Tracking IT Spend

Amid pandemics and economic downturns, companies are searching for every opportunity to cut costs. Squeezing the IT budget is a popular place to start. Over the years, IT organizations have reduced costs in operations, procurement and services by offshoring providers, consolidating data centers and moving services to the cloud. Nevertheless, additional savings and efficiencies are always possible by looking at opportunities to simplify and reduce complexity in the IT landscape. Referring back to the APQC discussion, IT and business leaders need to work together and align combined efforts with common capabilities and the company strategy to maximize investments. Since the EA organization has a unique perspective of the overall IT landscape, you are in excellent position to help control cost through increased standardization.

> *"Don't tell me where your priorities are. Show me where you spend your money and I'll tell you what they are." -- James W. Frick*

For the architect, traceable cost management does not need to be at the level of detail that would be used by financial controllers for cost control, but should be at a level that is easy to maintain and meaningful at the same time. There are two basic financial models that I like to measure company operations related to controlling cost. These are:

a) IT Budget Comparisons (IT Benchmarks)
b) Tracking Operational Expenses (Linking IT components to ongoing expenses to run day-to-day operations)

IT Budget Comparisons

A quick Internet search results in a number of quality IT Benchmark studies produced by companies like Gartner, McKinsey and IDC. Although IT Benchmark surveys are typically marketed for CFOs and CIOs, you can use these to develop a reference financial model to qualify a target state budget and staffing profile. In the context of the Living Enterprise Architecture, this information provides a high-level comparison of your IT performance to peer organizations who are also investing to enhance business outcomes and performance.

In the example below from Computer Economics (computereconomics.com)[5], they have provided a table analyzing IT spending as a percentage of revenue across several industries (Exhibit 31). By dividing your total IT budget by total revenue, number of employees, or number of desktops supported, you get an indicator of how your IT cost compares to industry peers.

IT Spending Ratios
Between 25th and 75th Percentiles, by Industry

IT Spend as...	Discrete Mfg	Fin'l Services	High Tech	Retail	Health care
Percentage of Revenue	1.4%- 3.2%	4.4%- 11.4%	2.6%- 4.7%	1.2%- 3.0%	3.0%- 5.9%
Per User	$3,733- $9,864	$13,772- $26,667	$6,191 - $11,653	$3,913- 14,685	$3,157- $6,143
Per Desktop/ Laptop	$4,658- $9,395	$12,171 - $23,882	$5,452- $9,218	$4,806- $13,533	$3,280- $7,273

Source Computer Economics, 2019

EXHIBIT 31: IT SPEND RATIOS BY INDUSTRY

For example, assume your company has the following profile:

- **Revenue = $1.85B**
- **Users = 8000**
- **Desktops = 9000**
- **Corporate IT Budget = $90M**

Plugging into Table 8, you can quickly see how your company compares to the industry averages for % of Revenue, IT cost per user and IT cost per desktop. With this benchmark in place, you are in great shape to understand your IT spending habits.

TABLE 8: IT SPEND EXAMPLE COMPARISON

IT Spend as..	Your Company	Discrete Mfg	Financial Service	High Tech	Retail	Healthcare
% of revenue	4.9%	1.4%-3.2%	4.4%-11.4%	2.6%-4.7%	1.2%-3%	3%-5.9%
Per User	$11,250	$3,733 - $9,864	$13,772 - $26,667	$6,191 - $11,653	$3,913 - $14,685	$3,157 - $6,143
Per Desktop	$9,000	$4,658 - $9,395	$12,171 - $23,882	$5,452 - $9,218	$4,806 - $13,533	$3,280 - $7,273

Tracking Operation Expenses

Every company has an IT architecture, but most do not control it. Without Architecture Principles in place to guide good decision making and a CMDB to inventory assets, the IT Landscape can organically grow with duplicative systems, inconsistent data and ad-hoc integrations. With many IT projects driven by short-term business wants rather than long-term IT/Business planning, the patchwork of IT systems becomes Swiss cheese for Security and IT operations to support and maintain. With the Living Architecture in place, you can now quickly answer cost management questions like:

- What is the cost of IT? Marketing? Sales?
- Are we investing according to strategy?

What is the Cost of IT?

With accurate hardware and software assets in the CMDB inventory, you can quickly dashboard and filter your costs by business unit, and stack rank top spenders and applications by department as shown in Exhibit 32.

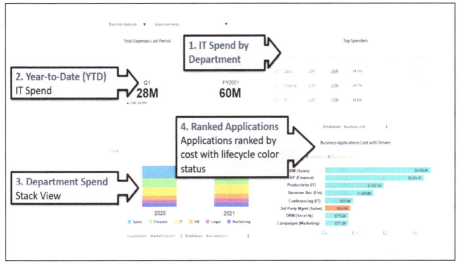

EXHIBIT 32: IT COSTS BY BUSINESS UNIT

Key points from Exhibit 32 are:

(1) Current IT expenses Year-to-Date (YTD).
(2) Department IT expenses YTD.
(3) Stack view of Department IT expenses YTD.
(4) Business applications ranked by license costs and color-coded based on application lifecycle. In this case, 'Green' is Production while 'Orange' is on the Retirement path.

Are we investing according to strategy?

As you recall from Chapter 6, all approved projects must pass through the IT Demand pipeline. As part of Demand justification, proposed projects need a business sponsor, budget and alignment to strategic objectives. Once approved and in-flight, you can use a dashboard similar to Exhibit 33 to track your IT Spend to strategy and benefits.

EXHIBIT 33: IT PROJECT SPEND TO STRATEGY

Key points from Exhibit 33 are:

(1) Current active projects and their planned budgets and actual costs. (Do you notice the similarities to EVM in Chapter 4?)
(2) Pie charts tracking projects to strategic benefits.
(3) Pie charts tracking project investment categories and priority

From the mapping of Applications to supporting Infrastructure, you can quickly gain insight on expected infrastructure savings (Exhibit 34). Conceptually, if something new is being added to the IT landscape, then one or more systems should be retired. By aggressively trying to simplify the digital ecosystem, we can reduce costs and better position IT to be flexible in meeting business change.

Mapping To Be Retired Applications to Infrastructure

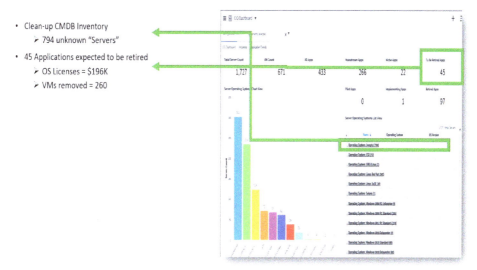

- Clean-up CMDB Inventory
  - 794 unknown "Servers"
- 45 Applications expected to be retired
  - OS Licenses = $196K
  - VMs removed = 260

EXHIBIT 34: IT APPLICATION TO INFRASTRUCTURE SPEND

Key points from Exhibit 34 are:

(1) The infrastructure inventory shows 794 unknown servers. This is a red flag and indicates shadow IT and/or bad inventory data. You should be identifying any IT assets 2+ versions behind current vendor offerings since these will be a security and maintenance risk.

(2) The dashboard also shows 45 applications expected to be retired. You want to monitor that these systems get decommissioned as planned. Many times, decommission dates get slipped which adds to the overall technical debt.

****

<u>Take-Away</u>

- ➢ The Living Architecture View allows you to control and clean-up the IT Architecture
  - ○ Standardize software licenses by consolidating capabilities to maximize investments and gain economies of scale.
  - ○ Retire, rationalize and decommission duplicative applications and systems.
  - ○ Cancel projects that are not aligned with company strategy.

****

PART FOUR – Parting Thoughts

I hope you enjoyed reading this book. Enterprise Architecture is an exciting profession. As a former colleague liked to say, *"We are on a journey."*, and as you continue forward, I want to leave you with a few parting thoughts on content that did not make it into the previous sections.

Inevitably at some point, a CFO is going to ask, "How much is Enterprise Architecture going to cost me?" What the CFO is asking is what does your staffing model look like and is anything capitalizable. Addressing staffing first, Enterprise Architects have unique skills combining technical knowledge, data analytics, and business acumen. Successful architects have expertise in a technology domain (business systems, data, applications, infrastructure), and also have excellent communication and presentation skills to lead discussions between technical SMEs and business roles. Plan on each architect to be able to lead 3-5 projects simultaneously depending on scope and size. When hiring, my recommendation is to hire an EA generalist for each technology domain architect hired (Exhibit 35).

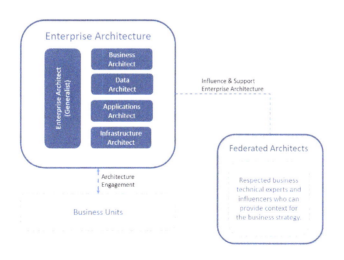

Exhibit 35: Architecture Staffing Model

Generalist are important because they have proven expertise within an architecture domain, but can also work across the broad IT spectrum, acting as sounding boards and thought leaders on other solution designs, whiteboards and assessments. Generalist provide flexibility to take on a number of assignments and demands.

To provide additional elasticity to the ebbs and flows of business demands, a "Federated Architecture" model is recommended to provide a dotted line between your organization and other departments who have individuals that can contribute in whiteboards and architecture materials. A Federated Architecture is important to open communication channels and information sharing between the Lines of Business (LOBs) and centrally hosted IT. Table 9 provides a description of each role.

TABLE 9: ARCHITECT ROLE DEFINITIONS

Domain Enterprise Architects	Domain Enterprise Architects support efforts for a specific domain, including defining how the domain fits into the Business/IT strategy.
Enterprise Architects (Generalist)	Enterprise Architects coordinate across domains. The manifestation of their work supports the overall business strategy.
Federated Architects	Federated Architects represent technology thought leaders within the business who have the ability to influence events that define business operations.
Busines Unit Solution Architects	Business Solution Architects are business technical staff with an expertise in critical business application functionality. These

	individuals were hired and report to the business.

Software capitalization involves the recognition of internally-developed software as a fixed asset. From the CFO's perspective, capitalized software is amortized instead of being expensed; therefore, lowering reported expenses and increasing company net income. Internal use software is identified as anything acquired or developed only for internal business needs. If you are using an enterprise architecture tool (and to be Level 4 CMMI compliant you should be) then cost incurred to purchase, develop, install and test the EA software tool can be capitalized. Any costs related to data conversion, user training, administration and overhead are charged to expense as incurred.

As discussed in Chapter 11, maintaining the Living Enterprise Architecture is an EA job function that requires diligence to inventory the IT portfolio and maintain its relationships. With an architecture tool in place, an individual is needed who is organized and skilled to routinely monitor and supervise the portfolio. This could be a fulltime or part-time position, but someone needs to be on point.

Finally, your biggest challenge in building and maintaining a successful EA practice is business commitment and buy in. Chapter 6 provides sound guidance on tactical execution, but committed support from the business is more rapidly achieved if the EA function reports directly to the CEO/CFO/COO. In a public company, the EA charter should come from the Board of Directors. Unfortunately, in most businesses, the EA function gets assigned to the CIO. This can make EA adoption an ongoing uphill battle for the CIO since there are no performance objectives from other functional executives to orient.

****

Take-Away

- ➤ To speed EA adoption across the organization and avoid uphill battles:
    - o The EA charter should come from the Board of Directors.
    - o EA should report directly to a Level 1 or Level 2 C-Suite executive (e.g. CEO, CFO, COO) to ensure cross-functional support.
- ➤ Enterprise Architecture software can be capitalized if the software is considered to be for internal use supporting the needs of the business.
- ➤ Public speaking and presentation skills are extremely import for architects to communicate ideas and influence audiences. Organizations like Toastmasters International® excel at providing a fun and supportive environment to develop and tune.presentation and leadership skills.

****

List of Abbreviations

AC	Actual Cost
APM	Application Portfolio Management
ARB	Architecture Review Board
BAC	Budget at Completion
BPA	Business Process Architecture
CAC	Cost at Completion
CBP	Capability Based Planning
CEO	Chief Executive Officer
CIO	Chief Information Officer
CMMI	Capability Maturity Model Integration
COBIT	Control Objectives for Information and Related Technology
CPI	Cost Performance Index
CTO	Chief Technical Officer
CV	Cost Variance
DA	Data Architecture
DNS	Domain Name Service
EA	Enterprise Architecture
EAC	Estimate at Complete
ERP	Enterprise Resource Planning
ETC	Estimate to Complete
EV	Earned Value
EVM	Earned Value Management
HR	Human Resources
IT	Information Technology
LOB	Line of Business
M&A	Merger & Acquisition
NOD	Notice of Decision
NPS	Net Promoter Score
OOTB	Out-of-the-Box
PCF	Process Classification Framework

PM	Project Manager
PMO	Project Management Office
POC	Proof of Concept
PV	Planned Value
RACI	Responsible, Accountable, Consulted and Informed
ROI	Return on Investment
SDD	Solution Design Document
SME	Subject Matter Expert
SPI	Schedule Performance Index
SV	Schedule Variance
TOGAF	The Open Group Architecture Framework
YTD	Year to Date

References

1. Jeanne W. Ross, Peter Weill, and David C. Robertson. (2006). *Enterprise Architecture as a Strategy*

2. Wardley, Simon. (2019, April 10). *Pioneers settlers and town planners* Wardleypedia.org, https://wardleypedia.org/mediawiki/index.php/Pioneers_settlers_town_planners

3. APQC, (October 31, 2017), *Process vs. Capability*, APQC.org, https://www.apqc.org/resource-library/resource-listing/process-vs-capability-understanding-difference

4. The Open Group, (2001, 2002, 2003), *Architecture Principles,* opengroup.org, https://pubs.opengroup.org/architecture/togaf80-doc/arch/p4/princ/princ.htm

5. Computer Economics, (2019), *IT Spending as a Percentage of Revenue by Industry, Company Size, and Region*, computereconomics.com, https://www.computereconomics.com/article.cfm?id=2626

About the Author

Russ Gibfried is a recognized IT leader and authority in the planning and delivery of IT business systems and strategies using Enterprise Architecture techniques. With more than three decades of technology experience, Russ is a seasoned executive with a track record of improving enterprise services that have boosted client competitive advantage and maximized value through growth and innovation. To each new initiative, Russ brings a pragmatic, approach and a relentless focus on driving customer value and satisfaction.

Russ has served as Director of Enterprise Architecture and Integration for Teradata when Teradata relocated its headquarters from Ohio to San Diego. There, Russ was responsible for establishing the Enterprise Architecture practice and achieving cost reductions through rationalizing their application portfolio and integration strategy. Prior to Teradata, Russ was with Hewlett Packard Enterprise (HPE) where he served as Chief Architect for HPE's State and Local division representing counties and state agencies in California. Previously, he also held leadership roles at Carefusion and SAIC helping execute their successful architecture programs.

Russ is a distinguished presenter on technology and enterprise architecture. Russ earned his BS in Mathematics from UC Santa Barbara. He is Enterprise Architecture Master Level 2 and TOGAF certified, as well as Azure Cloud Architecture and AWS Cloud Practitioner Essentials certified.

Outside of the office, Russ enjoys traveling, skiing and paragliding. He has a talent for languages with conversation abilities in German, Spanish and basic Mandarin.

Russ welcomes feedback, success stories and input on this book on how to enable business success through Enterprise Architecture. He is available as a speaker, consultant and workshop leader and can be reached directly through his web site at: http://www.successful-ea.com.